CW01023609

Embroidered Knot Gardens

Embroidered Knot Gardens

Owen Davies & Gill Holdsworth

BATSFORD

Owen Davies
To all past and present Apprentices of the Royal School of Needlework
– the most talented and creative artist embroiderers in the world.

Gill Holdsworth
To Dick and all our family.

First published in the United Kingdom in 2006 by
B T Batsford
151 Freston Road
London
W10 6TH

An imprint of Anova Books Company Ltd

ISBN-13 9780713489668
ISBN-10 0 7134 8966 9

A CIP catalogue record for this book is available from the British Library.

10 9 8 7 6 5 4 3 2 1

Reproduction by Anorax Imaging Ltd, Leeds
Printed and bound by CT Printing Ltd, China

This book can be ordered direct from the publisher at the website:
www.anovabooks.com, or try your local bookshop

Distributed in the United States and Canada by Sterling Publishing Co.,
387 Park Avenue South, New York, NY 10016, USA

CONTENTS

Introduction   6

1 Materials   8

2 Thinking about your design   14

3 Garden paths   36

4 Flowerbeds   48

5 Water features   70

6 Hedging and topiary   78

7 Brick walls   94

Appendix 1   110

Appendix 2   119

Recommended further reading   124

Suppliers   125

Recommended gardens to visit   126

Acknowledgements   127

Index   128

Introduction

This is a book for anyone who enjoys both gardens and needlework. At the beginning of the 21st century, faced with restlessness and uncertainty, the idea of a quiet and ordered garden in a safe, enclosed space is just as appealing to us as it was to our forebears during the tumultuous years of the 17th century. With a needle and thread, you can design and create your own magical three-dimensional garden. You might choose to follow traditional lines, or you might develop an entirely contemporary garden, incorporating the best ideas from past and present. We have concentrated mainly on the knot garden designs of the 16th and 17th centuries, but the same principles and techniques can be used to embroider a garden of any period, entirely from your own imagination.

Before you start on your adventure, be warned that creating a needlework garden is an addictive process and could take over much of your life! It is not a short-term project. We know many students who have worked on the same garden for several years, but this is because they have researched and developed ideas as they have progressed, and enjoyed experimenting with different techniques and materials until satisfied that their garden has come to full bloom.

For a start, you will need to visit real gardens as part of the research process. In Britain there is no shortage of these, from the many outstanding botanical gardens and those of grand country houses to the little gems that are opened once or twice a year under the National Gardens Scheme (see Recommended Gardens to Visit on page 126). Worldwide, it is not difficult to find fascinating botanical gardens and visiting schemes to private gardens now operate in many countries. You should go armed with a notebook and camera and immerse yourself in colours, shapes and textures, always considering how you can translate the reality of the garden into fabric and thread.

If you wish to create an historically accurate garden, you will need know a little of the history of gardens, including why and how designs changed over the centuries. The colours and textures of a late 16th-century garden, for example, would be different from those of today because of the range of plants available in each era, so it is important to know when certain plants became available to garden designers.

You do not need to be a very experienced stitcher to start your garden, as we explain the techniques step by step, showing you how to create various effects and exploring a variety of canvaswork stitches, ribbonwork, stumpwork and beading. We hope that

Above: Inspiration for Owen's knot gardens was provided by this beautifully worked, textured and embroidered box.

you will enjoy giving free rein to your imagination, creating some areas of your garden through an unconventional approach to embroidery.

This book evolved from a continuing series of workshops run by Owen Davies at the Royal School of Needlework, London, and other venues throughout Britain. It has been inspired by all those students who have attended the workshops and been so generous in sharing their ideas and enthusiasm, and we have tried to recapture the excitement and creativity generated by the atmosphere of the classes. Our book is about experimenting with ideas, self-expression and innovation, and to all of you we would say be brave, experiment, have confidence to do things differently and, most of all, have fun!

Owen Davies and Gill Holdsworth

1 Materials

Left: Be tempted to buy unusual threads whenever you can.

You love gardens and plants, your imagination is running riot with ideas and your fingers are itching to get started on creating your needlework garden. Just as with real gardening, good preparation is the key and you will need the correct equipment if you are to work efficiently. As you will be creating a potential heirloom, it is worth investing in the best quality materials you can afford. We list the basic requirements, but as your garden evolves you will discern what other exciting additions you will need in the way of beads, metallic fabrics, threads and accessories.

Your initial research equipment should include a notebook, pencil and camera. Once you start assembling your sewing equipment, include some extra canvas for the experimental sampler to run alongside your main project.

Slate frame

There are various types of embroidery frame and not all are suitable for a garden project. One of the best frames to use, referred to throughout this book as a slate frame, is of a type well documented as far back as the 1770s, though a similar style of frame has probably been in use for well over a thousand years. It is not known where the relatively recent term 'slate' frame originated. In the 16th century this type of frame known as a 'tent' frame, the word shortened from the term 'tenter', which was a wooden framework used for stretching cloth evenly after it had been woven.

It is essential to use a sturdy slate frame for your project. Although this is an expensive item, it is worth making this initial investment, as the frame will last a lifetime. A slate frame is a square frame comprising two rollers and two adjustable arms, fixed into the rollers by split pins to create an area of the size you require. Usually made of beech, a strong frame will keep your work taut for a long period of time and prevent your canvas from becoming skewed as you work. Framing up a canvas properly will take about two hours; details on how to do this are included in Appendix 1. Remember that before you frame up you must first mark your design on the canvas.

Frame supports

Ideally, while you work your frame should be supported on trestles that can be adjusted to your height. However, many of us do not have enough domestic space to house these. Some frames are set on a stand so that they can be stored vertically and tipped horizontal while you are working. Alternatively, you can improvize by using a table of the correct height to support one side of your frame and an adjustable ironing board for the other.

Ring frame

It is essential to keep an experimental stitch sampler running alongside your main project and this can be worked on a ring frame. We suggest that you use a 25cm (10in) ring frame of the type that has a dowel that can be inserted into a stand or clamp, allowing you to work with both hands free.

Right: A range of canvases suitable for garden projects – the count of your canvas will affect the appearance of your design.

Below left: Make sure the slate frame is well supported and at the correct height for you while you work.

Below: It takes about two hours to secure the canvas correctly in the frame.

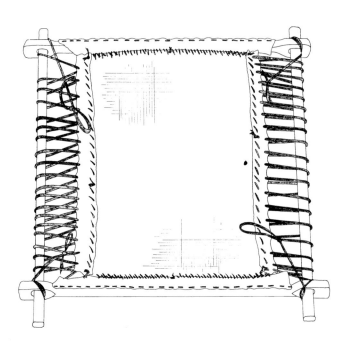

Canvas

Good quality canvas is a must for all the techniques to be used in this project. Aida will not be strong enough and neither will evenweave linens. There are three types of canvas available:

1] Mono canvas – a basic canvas, this is structured with single warp (lengthwise) threads and weft (widthwise) threads forming an even grid. The structure of the canvas tends to move so it is important that the whole piece should be held at even tension. Mono canvas is the type recommended for a garden project.

2] Interlock canvas – this single canvas is structured in the same way as mono, but with each square sewn through and 'locked'. This helps those unfamiliar with working on canvas, as it holds the tension and avoids the work becoming skewed if you are not using a slate frame. However, it is not recommended for use when stitching a garden project, for which a slate frame is a necessity.

3] Double canvas – here, a double line of canvas threads are used for the warp and weft. The double line can be split to accommodate two very fine stitches where one larger one would sit on a single canvas. This type of canvas is not necessary for a garden project.

All canvas is sized by the number of threads woven per inch (the count) and the range of threads per inch is 10, 12, 14, 16, 18, 22, 24. Size 10, the largest count (with the threads most widely spaced), has the lowest number of threads per inch and will result in large stitches. This is not really suitable for a garden project unless you are prepared to stitch a second time to make small stitches over the large ones.

Sizes 18 to 24 are the sizes most recommended for a garden project, because you can either achieve very fine detail with delicate threads in the small grid holes, or you can make bigger stitches by working individual stitches over a number of grid holes. Remember – be brave – experiment!

The count of your canvas will affect the appearance of your design: the same stitch used on a large count will give a completely different effect when worked on canvas of a finer count. Use your sampler to experiment beforehand and see how the same stitch, when worked on different sizes of canvas, can result in a range of completely different moods.

Colour of canvas

Canvas is usually either white or antique. Avoid using white canvas, as this base colour may show through your final work, especially if you have used textured threads. The brown antique, which is similar to the colour of soil, is preferable. The finer counts of canvas, 22 and 24, are sometimes available in peach or yellow, and these colours are also acceptable.

Needles

Discard the rule book and use whatever size of needle is suitable for the type of thread you are using at the time. For example, if you are using a chunky chenille or knitting yarn on canvas with a fine count, use a pointed needle with the biggest eye you can find, such as a large yarn darner. This will push down on the weave of the canvas and open a path for the yarn to run through, thus keeping the yarn in good condition while you work and preventing it from becoming worn or fluffy. If you are using very fine thread, choose a fine embroidery needle. You do not have to use blunt tapestry needles just because you are working on canvas; with pointed needles, you will find that it is easier to achieve the effects you are aiming for. Be brave, experiment!

Threads

Conventionally, wool or a combination of wool and silk is used for canvas work. However, when you are creating a three-dimensional garden, any combination of textured threads can be used to enhance your design and construct individual features. Be tempted to buy those unusual threads when you see them at a show or in a craft shop and have confidence to experiment with new concepts. If you are just starting to embroider and are uncertain what would work well, we offer suggestions throughout the book – but remember, too, that a garden stitched simply in crewel wool and stranded cottons can be very effective.

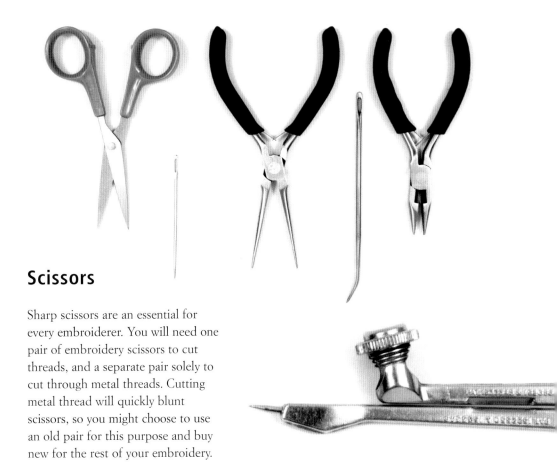

Scissors

Sharp scissors are an essential for every embroiderer. You will need one pair of embroidery scissors to cut threads, and a separate pair solely to cut through metal threads. Cutting metal thread will quickly blunt scissors, so you might choose to use an old pair for this purpose and buy new for the rest of your embroidery.

When you reach the stage of cutting the hedges, you will probably need to invest in sharp scissors with longer blades than those of normal embroidery scissors, but make sure they sit well in your hand and can easily be manipulated.

Lighting

Always try to ensure that you work in good light. Natural daylight is the most desirable light, but artificial daylight is a good second, so you may wish to invest in an Anglepoise or similarly adjustable lamp with a daylight bulb.

Designing

You will need graph paper and tracing paper (90gsm), sharp pencils and a pencil sharpener, a fine black waterproof pen, a compass, a metal rule and a tape measure. A light box is a very useful piece of equipment for transferring the design, but if you do not wish to purchase one and cannot borrow one from a friend, you can improvize with a glass top table and a lamp.

For details of suppliers see page 125 or, for frequently updated information, go to www.embroideredknotgardens.com.

2 Thinking about your design

Many of the readers of this book will find at least one famous garden somewhere very near them. Visit it, and as many other gardens as you can, to get the feel of garden design throughout the ages and to immerse yourself in changing seasonal colours and textures. Inspiration does not always come from famous gardens – don't forget to look at your own and your neighbours' gardens or visit your local park, where you may find the planting and shapes of the flowerbeds give you just what you are looking for. Take a notebook or sketchbook and camera, and remember to keep records of the gardens you have visited and at what season. Postcards, especially aerial views, can also be helpful.

It may take you a while to decide on the final design. You might narrow your research to a particular historical period or even re-create a specific garden. We concentrate on 16th- and 17th-century designs in this book, but you may wish to invent a garden that incorporates historical design principles interspersed with contemporary ideas of your own – for example, a knot filled with vegetables rather than flowers – or you may decide to create something entirely novel and individual for the 21st century.

Another idea would be to create a maze or labyrinth, either for the entire garden or for a quarter section of it. Conventionally, a labyrinth has only one path to the centre, albeit a very convoluted one. A maze offers a choice of direction at many points along the way (if you are thinking of creating a hedge maze, we suggest you read Chapter 6, Hedging and Topiary first). The other options are to make a maze or labyrinth with a path of canvas stitches.

Remember that you can find potential design shapes anywhere you look and inspiration often strikes when you least expect it. Knotted designs, especially, can often be found on plasterwork, woodwork, jewellery and embroidery. Printed textiles and wallpaper can also provide a myriad of ideas.

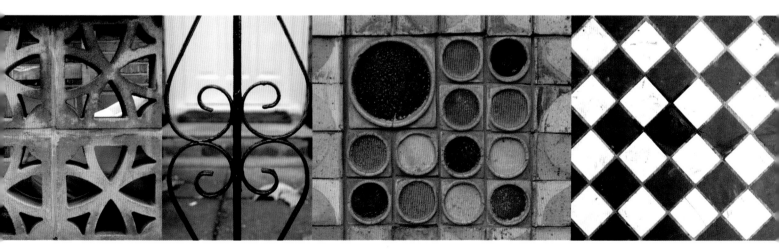

It can be fun to look at your own household objects with new eyes. Find a sympathetic friend and tour both your households, picking out shapes and patterns that might suggest new design ideas. The design shown here was taken from the carved wooden acanthus pattern on the door of a Victorian sideboard. This piece of furniture had been taken for granted in my dining room for years until Owen spotted its potential for a knot garden design. Alternatively, if you are uncertain where to start, you might like to try the design ideas we have given on pages 18–19.

Left: Inspiration for designs can be found in unexpected places.

Stage 1: Trace directly from the original photograph.

Stage2: Simplify the design to open up areas.

Stage 3: Basic line drawing of the design.

Stage 4: Begin marking areas for hedging, water feature and planting.

Above and left: Knot garden designs
that can be used or adapted for
your own projects.

Also, consider the complexity of your design in relation to your degree of experience as a needle worker. If you are a relative beginner, make sure your design is 'open', with fairly large areas for the flowerbeds, which will make them easier to work. Follow the pattern of an open 'parterre' garden rather than a complicated woven knot, and remember that your design does not have to be very complicated – a simple image can be very effective and satisfying.

Once you have decided on the main outlines of your design, think about the season in which your garden will be set. This important decision will determine some of the species of plants you choose to include and will affect your colour palette and the mood of your garden.

Below: Possible planting ideas.

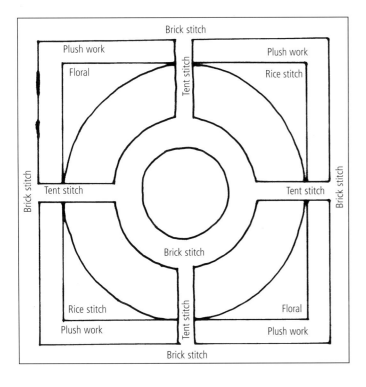

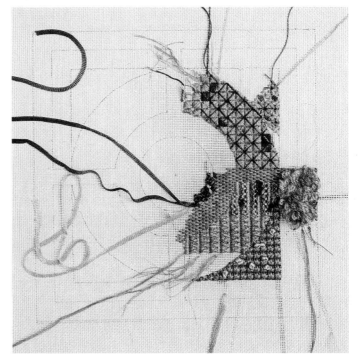

Above: Simplicity of design can be
very effective.

You will have been collecting sketches and photographs and aerial views of gardens that inspire you. To pull your final design ideas together, it can be helpful to bring all your images of inspirational gardens, artefacts, shapes and colour swatches together onto a storyboard.

While you are thinking about colour, also bear in mind where you intend to place the finished garden in your home. Surely it isn't going to live forever in a drawer or cupboard? Knot gardens come in various sizes and can have many uses, such as being set into the top of a functional box, as well as being solely decorative. However, if you are going to make a dramatic gesture and have your finished garden mounted in a glass-topped table in the centre of your sitting room, make sure it will connect with the rest of your décor.

Above: An inspirational storyboard for a knot garden design.

Below: A large tassel inspired by topiary in a knot garden.

So much work goes into the creation of an embroidered knot garden that we always think of it in terms of being a future heirloom. With this in mind, make sure you keep a written record of how you set about working your garden – what gave you the original idea and how you planned and designed it. You could record the threads you used and note how many hours it took you to create the garden from start to finish. Try to incorporate some form of personal feature into your garden, such as a representation of a favourite plant, or an initial on a wall or path, and again leave an explanation as to why you have done this. Owen stitched the names of his nieces, his three little roses, on the outside of the wall of his original knot garden and a family tree on the inside of the wall.

We recommend that throughout this project you make an experimental sampler of trial stitches alongside the main project, keeping this for posterity along with your written records. You may believe that no member of your family is really interested in what you are doing today, but just remember that future generations will be fascinated by your work. Imagine how thrilled you would be if you came across an embroidery stitched a hundred or so years ago by a great-grandparent or a great aunt, or even a known friend of the family, and you also had written and stitched records to explain the background of the piece.

- Graph paper
- Heavy duty tracing paper (90gsm)
- Sharp pencil (HB)
- Pencil sharpener
- Metal ruler
- Compass, for circles and arcs
- Fine black waterproof pen, such as Staedtler 001
- Tape to secure both design and canvas to a light surface
- Access to a light box, if possible

Left: A contemporary design based on Karl Rushen's award-winning garden at the Chelsea Flower Show, London.

Transferring the design to canvas

Planning an accurate design and transferring it accurately onto the canvas is probably the most important step in creating your knot garden.

If you are creating a very traditional knot garden, remember that a conventional design should be symmetrical, with the four corners presenting mirror images radiating from a central feature. However, if you want to avoid tradition, have the confidence to do things differently and adapt the garden to your own specifications, as in the acanthus design inspired by the Victorian sideboard (see pages 16–17). You can also have different flowerbed layouts in each quarter, if you prefer.

Work out the width(s) of your paths to ensure that the proportions of paths to flowerbeds are pleasing to your eye. Bear in mind what count of canvas you will be using and how many stitches you will need to cover the width of each path. An even number of stitches across a path looks better, but remember that if the path is next to a hedge, you will lose sight of one stitch along the edge of the path as the hedge foliage will overhang it. You will find it helpful to work a little sample of path first to get an idea of the number of stitches required for your proposed width of path (see pages 43–47 for stitches for paths). At the same time, you can experiment with colour combinations. Although you should aim to be as accurate as possible in your initial drawing, don't try to be too mathematically technical when working out proportions – have confidence to rely on your own reaction to what pleases you.

It is important to keep your final master line drawing until you have completed stitching your garden. You may need to refer to your design ideas throughout, and you will find it particularly useful to have the intended placing of your hedging clearly marked when, right at the end, you come to stitch and then clip the plushwork areas.

Draw the outline of your garden on graph paper and check that the garden you envisage fits the size of the canvas comfortably, leaving at least 10cm (4in) all around to allow for framing up and mounting the finished piece. At this stage, check that your canvas will fit your slate frame (see page 111) and find the centre point of your canvas as follows: first, make sure your canvas is cut accurately on the grain, both horizontally and vertically. Measure along the top and bottom of the canvas, find the centre points and mark these accurately with a pencil. Now measure along each side and mark those centre points. Using a firm ruler (preferably one with a metal edge), draw a pencil line from the centre points, first from top to bottom and then across. The point at which the two lines cross will be the centre of the canvas. Check that your pencil lines really

are straight and on the grain of the canvas before marking a central cross, about 1.5cm (½in) in each direction, with a fine waterproof pen.

Now begin to draw the full design on graph paper as accurately as you can, ensuring that your pencil remains sharp. Draw all straight lines against a ruler and use a compass for circles and arcs. It is worth spending time getting the drawing correct at this stage, so you have a crisp, sharp and accurate pencil drawing at the end of the exercise. When you are completely satisfied with the design, go over the pencil lines with a fine black pen. Also find and mark the exact centre point of your design so that you can marry it up on the canvas.

Transferring the design to canvas is a tricky step and will be greatly helped if you have access to a light box. Tape the design onto the light box and then cover it with the canvas, making sure you accurately match up the centre points and keeping the canvas grain straight on the design. Tape the canvas securely and then, following the illuminated lines underneath, draw the design on the canvas in pencil, using your ruler and compass where necessary to maintain the accuracy of the design. If you do not have a light box, try using a glass-topped table with a lamp placed underneath.

Once your design is drawn on the canvas, you are ready to frame up (see page 112).

Choosing stitches

At the start of your project, it is probably difficult to know which stitches you will use to create the desired effect. Be prepared for your choice of stitches and techniques to change and develop as you work the garden – it's rather like real gardening, where you can constantly experiment with planting plans while the work is in progress. From the beginning, it is very useful to stitch an experimental sampler alongside your main project. The sampler can be worked on a ring frame and you can use it in the first instance while you are calculating a pleasing width for your pathways and experimenting with the number of stitches across your path.

Before you commit needle to canvas on your main project, it is also helpful to see the effect various textures of thread will have: the same stitch can have a completely altered appearance and lend itself to a variety of moods when worked in different types of thread, or even different colours. You will find suggestions for various stitches to suit different areas of the garden in the subsequent chapters.

Historical background

The accession of Henry VII to the throne in 1485, following the Wars of the Roses, resulted in a period of peace and prosperity in England. Henry VIII led a fashion for new building work and creating imaginative gardens that incorporated the ideas on garden design that were filtering through from Italy and France. The garden at Hampton Court Palace, created during the 1530s, was considered extremely innovative with its carved and painted beasts, its use of coloured sand – and its knots.

Tudor gardens were filled with symbolism, and the knot has been used as a symbol from the earliest civilizations. There are examples of interlaced designs on Sumerian carvings dating from the third millennium BC. Roman mosaic designs frequently contain complex interwoven patterns. Examples of knots as a symbol of love appear in Renaissance paintings and today we still speak of 'tying the knot' in relation to marriage. During the course of some marriage ceremonies, couples are still symbolically tied together with fabric.

Knot gardens remained popular for about 100 years from the 1530s, but their popularity began slowly to decline from the middle of the 17th century. With the 18th-century vogue for landscaping and the cult of Capability Brown, most Renaissance knots in England were destroyed. Today we only have re-creations of what we think the original knot gardens may have looked like; the present knot garden at Hampton Court, for example, was re-created by Ernest Law in the 1920s.

Right: Knot gardens at Hatfield House, Hertfordshire.

A celebration of colour

The way we use colour is vital to our overall perception of the embroidered garden. Colour is a subjective concept and we all see light and shade differently. We each have preferred colours for different purposes – sometimes this preference is by individual choice and sometimes it is dictated by social convention or fashion. We are all attracted to our own perception of beauty and this is reflected in our colour choice of clothes and jewellery, and the colours with which we surround ourselves in our homes.

If you have always been cautious in your use of colour, embroidering a garden can give you an opportunity to experiment with ideas you would not normally consider. Using your sampler, work examples of colour jüxtapositions to discover which you find pleasing and which will evoke the atmosphere you are aiming for. Look at the variety of shades in the images on pages 29–35. All these shades could be used for various areas of your embroidered garden.

Choosing the right colour range will be one of the keys to successfully completing the project and the choice of colours available may seem overwhelming when you start seriously thinking about it. If this is your first garden, try to keep to a fairly simple palette. Also, it will help to choose one category from the time of day, for example morning, midday, evening or midnight and a season, such as spring, summer, autumn or winter. This will focus your ideas on colour choice and the mood of your garden. For example a morning garden in the spring will evoke fresh colours such as lime greens and yellows while a morning garden in the winter brings to mind hard frost-encrusted soil using dark browns and white.

The colours you choose for the embroidered garden will have the same effect on the eye as a planting scheme in a garden. Of course, the real beauty with this garden is that planting comes but once and lasts a lifetime. Do not be afraid of making mistakes – sometimes they can enhance your work in unexpected ways. The theory and use of colour is a wide subject which we are not able to explore in detail here, but we offer some pointers for the use of different shades.

Complementary colours

Colours which appear opposite one another on a colour wheel are known as complementary colours and will work well together. Green and red are complementary colours, as are orange and blue and yellow and violet. Pink and hot pink shades work very well mixed in borders with red, yellow, green, blue and violet.

White

White, which comes in a variety of shades, can be introduced to highlight areas, to have a calming effect, especially when mixed with shades of green, and to be a foil to other colours. In a winter garden the hedges and topiary take a darker, more sinister look next to white borders. A midnight garden, with a full moon bathing the plants in eerie half light, takes on new interesting shades and shapes. White works very well with this concept.

Green

Throughout the seasons the staple colour is green. Many of the stitches in the flowerbeds are broken down into two parts representing foliage and flower. The shade of green you use as foliage colour will influence the shade of the bloom, so experiment to find the best combinations. The photos above show a small selection of greens available to the stitcher and gardener.

Red

Red is a welcome highlight in a garden, initially evoking a hot summer garden. Use red in association with orange and yellow to generate a feeling of vibrant warmth, but use it subtly as it can be a powerfully overwhelming shade. Red, however, can also symbolize the start of autumn and a cooling down of the soil.

Blue

Blue is one of the best-loved colours in the garden, and has a variety of shades. Although blue can be carried right through the seasons, in spring it really begins to come into its own. In the seasonal garden, rice stitch and lapis lazuli stones are used to create a rich flowerbed. A garden is not complete without some hint of blue. Even small specks next to yellow are effective, and orange and blue are complementary colours (see above).

Orange

Orange is a shade avoided by many stitchers, which is a pity as this can blaze gloriously, especially when combined with emerald green. These photos demonstrate the additional colours that can be found beside a main shade. A garden stitched with orange and yellow, with a slight hint of pink, will be tipped towards the higher scale of hot.

Violet

Violet is best suited to spring or early summer gardens. The photos show a variety of different shades. On some, the greens surrounding the flower create a rich jade background, while violet and yellow are also complementary colours (see above).

Yellow

Yellow brings all the seasons together. It's the most common colour used in embroidered knot gardens and looks stunning mixed with the complementary colour, violet. Yellow reflects more light than any other colour. It can be placed in a flowerbed with the subtle approach and yet still our eyes are drawn to it.

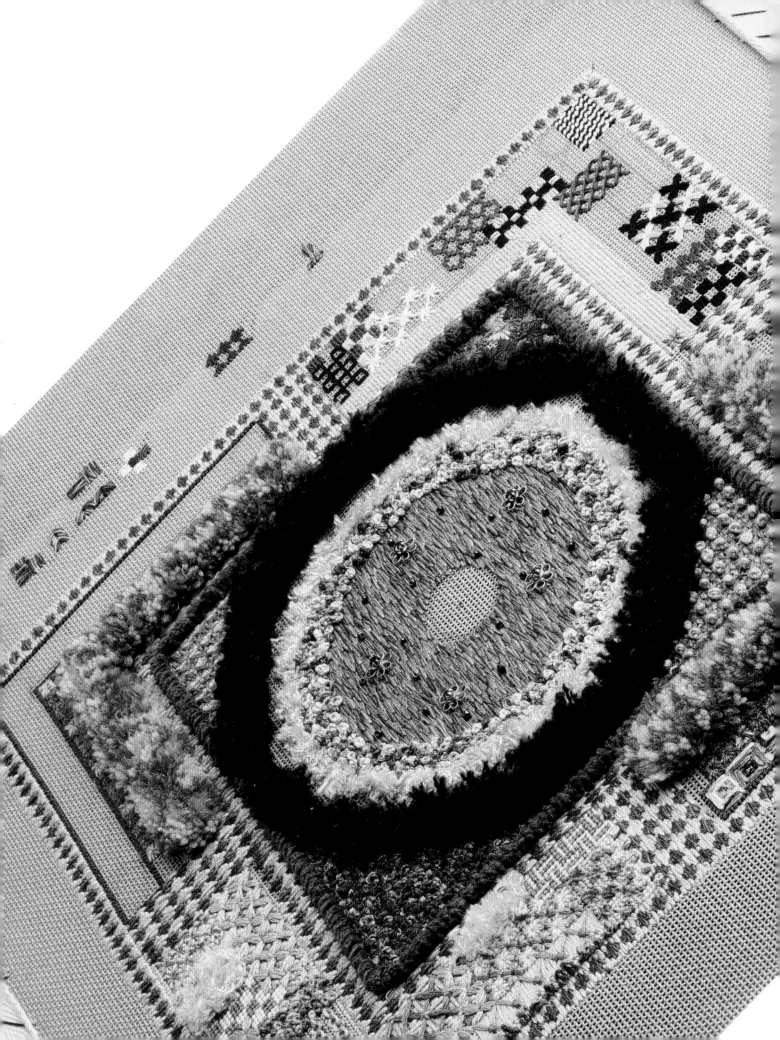

3 Garden paths

Paths form the foundation of your design and should be worked first. Not all designs will necessarily have paths running across the garden. Conventionally, however, all should have one running square around the edge, either filling the gap between the flowerbeds and the boundary wall or hedge or at the inner edge of the flowerbeds that abut the boundary.

Paths can be worked in a number of ways. You might use a variety of canvas stitches or French knots, for example, or you can work the same stitch used to create the brick walls and so create a warm, brick-effect path (see page 102).

Stranded cotton is the best thread to use for a stitched path as it gives a good, solid appearance. Wool can look too fluffy and unrealistic. The number of strands in the needle will vary with the size of the canvas.

You may wish to use real stones to create crazy paving. It is possible to purchase small pebbles with holes drilled in the centre. When you attach these to the canvas your stitch will obviously show, but you can use textured thread to create interesting effects of small plants and algae growing in the gaps.

A path can also be covered in a piece of material, such as a textured fabric or suede. Note that this technique is probably suitable only for the more experienced stitcher because of the added complication to the framing up process, as described overleaf.

Above and left: Paths provide a foundation of geometric patterns to give interest and solidity to the garden.

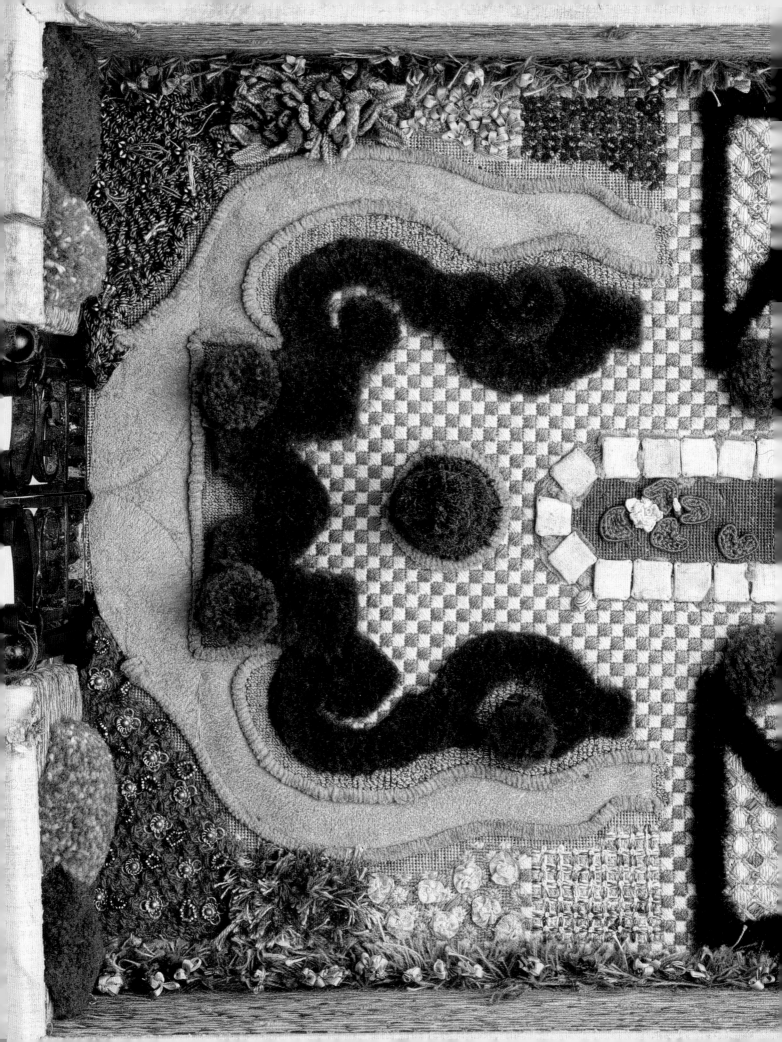

- A piece of suede sufficiently large for you to cut each segment of path to the required length and width
- Gutermann thread in a shade to match the suede
- Sharp chenille needle
- Sharp scissors to cut the suede
- A soft graphite pencil
- The original tracing of your design
- A hard, firm surface on which to transfer the design to the suede

Applying a suede path

A suede path, or indeed any kind of fabric path, should be the very first artefact you create in your garden, applied before you place any stitches on the canvas. This is because any fabric that is to lie on top of canvas should be applied on a slack frame. In this way, the canvas and the fabric can ultimately be tightened up together to the same tension. If you know you are going to apply suede, therefore, you should leave the canvas slack while you are framing up (see page 116). However, if your fabric path is a late decision, you can slacken the string along the frame arms so the canvas is still firm, with not too much movement, but not taut.

Take the original tracing of your design and turn it over so that the back faces you. With the soft pencil, trace over the areas of the required paths. Now put the suede on a hard surface, turn the tracing right way up and place it on the suede. Taking great care that the suede does not move, draw over the front of the design of the path areas on your tracing. When you remove the tracing, the graphite from the back will have been transferred to the suede, which will now show the faint outlines of the path.

Carefully re-draw these outlines with the soft pencil, drawing directly on the suede, and then cut out the path shapes with sharp scissors.

Right: Suede blocks and satin stitch over card create pebbles on a suede-based path.

Far right: Suede path with chenille-covered wire edging.

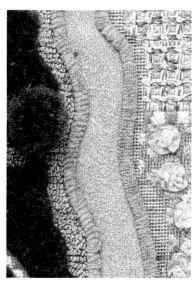

Now apply the suede to the appropriate areas of the design on your canvas; the strips should fit perfectly. Thread the chenille needle and secure the suede to the canvas, using tiny stab stitches. Bring the needle up just outside the suede edge and take it down approximately 1mm (½in) inside the edge of the fabric.

Once you are certain that you have applied all the suede or other fabric strips to the design, tighten up the frame to a good, taut tension.

Versatile canvas stitches

Canvas work, especially when worked in a fine tent stitch, is often erroneously called 'tapestry', but true tapestry is woven on a loom while canvas work is stitched with a needle. Tent stitch, sometimes referred to as petit point, is one of the smallest canvas stitches and is worked over just one intersection of the canvas. It can be used anywhere in the garden for paths, flowerbeds or water.

One of the delights of embroidering a knot garden, however, is that it gives you the opportunity to experiment with a wide variety of canvas stitches. Both paths and flowerbeds can be created solely with the imaginative use of canvas stitches. Although it is fun to use other techniques and a mixture of materials to create plants, water features and other effects, canvas stitches will form the bedrock of the garden.

At this stage it is worth describing how all canvas stitches are started and finished off.

Right: Clever use of canvas stitches result in a colourful and varied garden design.

Starting

Thread your needle and tie a knot in the end of the wool or stranded cotton, making sure that it is sufficiently large not to be pulled through the hole of the canvas. Decide where on the canvas you are going to start stitching. Find a place on the canvas about 3.5cm (1½in) away from your starting place and plunge the needle through the canvas, taking it from the top to the underneath so that the knot stays on the front of the canvas. Make sure that the area between the knot and the point where you will start to stitch will be covered by the stitches you are about to create (1). Take the needle behind and across to the starting point, pull it through to the front and begin. As you work, the 3.5cm (1½in) length of cotton or wool behind the canvas will be trapped by the stitches you make, providing you are working in the direction of the knot (2). When you reach the original knot on top of the canvas, carefully cut if off.

Finishing

When the yarn you are using becomes too short or begins to look worn, take it up through the canvas from below about 3.5cm (1½in) from where you are working and ahead of the direction of stitching (3). Leave the loose wool lying on top of the canvas and its length underneath will be trapped by the next stitches you create (4). Once you reach the place where the loose thread exits the canvas, carefully cut it off on the top.

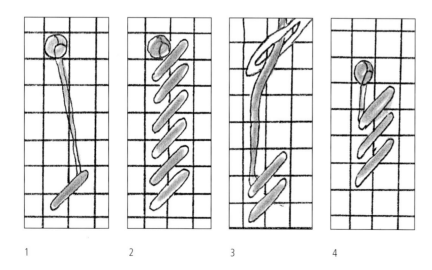

1   2   3   4

Canvas stitches for paths

A tale of two stitches: tent stitch and half cross stitch

Tent stitch, sometimes referred to as 'petit point', is one of the smallest canvas stitches and worked over just one diagonal intersection of the canvas. It is a useful basic stitch that can be used anywhere in the garden for paths, flowerbeds or water. Many embroiderers confuse tent stitch with half cross stitch because both stitches look the same on the surface. However, although related, these are worked differently and must not be interchanged.

Tent stitch uses twice as much yarn as half cross stitch and so creates a substantial, hard wearing stitch that is commonly used for chair covers and cushions. The extra length of yarn is carried at the back of the stitch.

Both stitches are worked in rows across the diagonal of the canvas threads, but whereas tent stitch is always started from the upper row of the canvas downward, half cross stitch is begun from the second row (see the digrams overleaf).

A frequent mistake is that the first row of stitching left to right is worked in tent stitch, and the return journey right to left is worked in half cross stitch. Although the stitches appear the same on top, the different lengths of yarn between the stitches at the back of the work will create an uneven tension, which will eventually skew the canvas and distort the embroidery.

For the knot garden, it really does not matter which stitch you use as long as you keep to the same one all the way through.

Above: From the front of the canvas, tent stitch and half cross stitch appear the same. Turn to the back of the canvas to reveal their differences.

Tent stitch

Start at the left on the upper row of two horizontal rows. Bring the needle up at 1 and down at 2. Pass the needle diagonally underneath and come up at 3 and down at 4. You will have a long diagonal stitch at the back between 2 and 3. Continue along the row in the same way.

When you reach the end of the row, take the needle underneath from 16 down vertically under one canvas thread to come up at 17. Bring the needle down at 18 and up again at 19 and work your way back along the row right to left. Again, you will see that you have a long diagonal stitch at the back between 18 and 19.

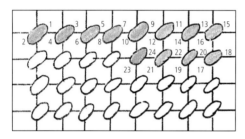

Front view

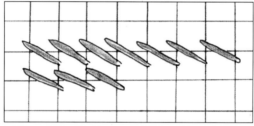

Back view

Half cross stitch

Begin at the left on the lower row of two horizontal rows. Bring the needle up at 1 and down at 2. Drop down one canvas thread to the hole below 2 and come up at 3 and down at 4. You will have a short vertical stitch at the back between 2 and 3. When you reach the end of the row at 16, take the needle behind vertically down under one canvas thread to 17. Take the needle across one diagonal canvas thread to 18, up at 19 and down at 20. You will have a short vertical stitch at the back between 18 and 19.

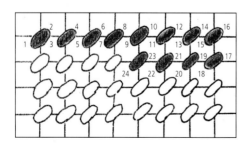

Front view

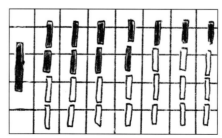

Back view

Cushion or cushion variation stitch

A variety of square stitches can be used for paths, but a good one to start with is cushion stitch (also know as Scottish stitch). A variation, cushion reverse stitch, can be worked by working one colour on a diagonal running from bottom right to top left and the other colour, in the adjacent square, running diagonally in the opposite direction to achieve a dramatic effect.

If you are working on a 24-count canvas, you will need a size 24 needle and 6 strands of cotton in the needle. If you are working on a larger count of canvas, you will need more strands in the needle.

The stitch forms a diagonal pattern using five stitches and you can vary the size of the square by working over three, five or seven threads of canvas, or even more if you require really big squares. The stitch illustrated below uses five stitches over three canvas threads.

To work over three threads, start at the top left of the first square. Bring your needle up at 1 and down at 2. Drop the needle down to the next row below to come up at 3 and down at 4. Come up at 5 to form the longest stitch of the square taking the needle down at 6. Repeat the process, reducing the stitch down from steps 7 to 10.

Stitch the next square in the contrasting colour, either running in the same direction or, to work the reverse stitch variation, with the stitches running on the opposite diagonal. Now you have your two first 'master' stitches in place, you can stitch in one colour diagonally down the canvas and then return and complete the other colour on the adjacent diagonal.

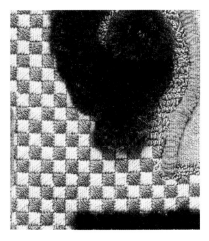

Above: Cushion stitch is an effective block stitch for paths.

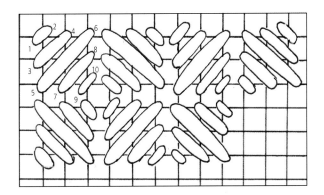

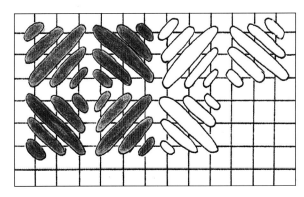

Hungarian stitch

Hungarian stitch gives an attractive tile effect, which is useful if you are considering a Moorish garden or one with a very contemporary design. If you are an inexperienced stitcher, however, we recommend that you use only one colour for this stitch, as the placing of each row of stitches can be tricky. The sets of three stitches in each stitch group drop down alternately but remain interlinked to the group above. If you make a mistake in placing a stitch of a different colour, it will be very obvious and will have to be unpicked.

The stitch comprises three vertical stitches, two smaller ones to the left and right of a longer one, but the longer stitch is placed so that it also interlocks with the two smaller stitches of the rows above and below.

You will work each set of three from left to right, alternately dropping down diagonally to the row below, and then returning to the original row. Decide where the top of the tile stitching will be on the canvas and drop down four clear holes from there. Starting with the first small stitch on the left at 1, bring the needle up from behind and pass it up vertically, taking it straight over two canvas threads so the cotton in the needle covers one hole. Plunge the needle down behind the canvas at 2 and then move it towards the right to the next vertical row. Pass the needle down behind and over three canvas threads so it comes up in the hole which is diagonally one down from the beginning of the first stitch at 3. Pass the needle up over four threads so that three holes are covered by the cotton. Plunge down again at 4 and move the needle towards the right. Pass the needle behind over three threads so it comes up in the hole which is level with the beginning of the first stitch at 5. Again, pass the needle over two canvas threads and plunge it down so that the third stitch is exactly the same size and level with the first stitch at 6. The first set of Hungarian stitch is now complete.

Right: Hungarian stitch provides an attractive tile effect.

- Stranded cotton – the number of strands used in the needle depend on the count of the canvas and the desired thickness of the texture of the path (you can use different shades of the same colour in the needle, but ensure that you keep to the same combination throughout)
- Tapestry needle appropriate to the count of the canvas

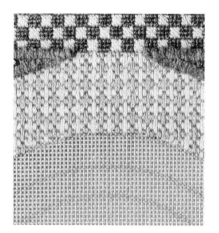

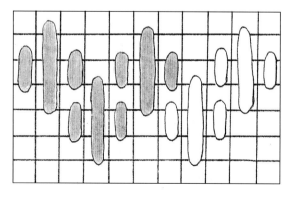

To work the second set, keep on the same vertical row and drop down behind the canvas over four threads. Bring the needle up at 7, pass the cotton over two canvas threads and plunge the needle back down through the same hole as used by the beginning of the third original stitch (8). Continue as for the first set 9, 10, 11, 12.

Once you have completed the second set, to return to the original row above for the third set, stay on the same vertical line of canvas and take your needle up behind the canvas over two threads. Bring the needle up at 13 and take it down across two threads on the top of the canvas. Plunge the needle through the same hole as the end of the third stitch of the second set (14).

Now move to the right and drop down behind over one thread, bringing the needle up on the same level as the original second stitch in the first set. Continue 15, 16, 17, 18 and then move on to 19, 20 to drop down to the lower row. Continue in the same way.

French knots for gravel

French knots are simple and fun to work and they make a very effective gravel path. For instructions on how to make French knots see page 60.

Brickwork stitch

For a stitch to make brick paths see page 102.

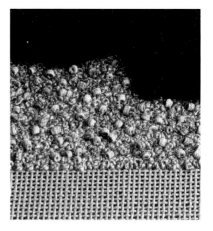

Top: French knots incorporating terracotta beads.

Above: French knots have been stitched around suede cut tiles.

Left and far left: Brickwork and mortar stitches (pages 102–103) create rustic paths.

4 Flowerbeds

It is often difficult to decide what stitches to include, but as you work, your ideas of which stitch to use in each of the flowerbeds will develop. It may help you to draw up a 'planting plan' of stitches as in the example given on page 20.

We have suggested a number of suitable canvas stitches, plus some simple stumpwork and ribbonwork techniques.

Canvas stitches

A remarkable range of canvas stitches is available to you. Remember you can use a variety of types of thread, and you can mix colours in the needle to variegate the effect in the petals. Browse through books of canvas stitches and you will be spoiled for choice, but remember always to work a sample first so you can get the 'feel' of a stitch and see how it looks on the size of canvas you have chosen to use. Remember, too, that you can alter the size of the stitch to fit the circumstances of the garden. If a stitch is conventionally worked over four canvas threads, for example, there is no reason why you cannot increase the distance in multiples of the same number, so you could work the same stitch over four, eight or twelve threads.

Unless the stitch is worked in rows that require a clear path, such as fan stitch or tent stitch, it is best to begin stitching in the middle of the flowerbed and work outwards. If you are halfway through a stitch when you come to the edge of the design line, just finish the stitch off as best you can and stop by the line.

We have concentrated first on a few stitches that can be broken down into at least two sections. One section can be worked in foliage shades and the other in colours to denote the flower.

Left: Textured flowerbeds using metal thread and canvas stitches.

Houndstooth

The main structure of this stitch is worked with diagonal green foliage bars running across the canvas. Start at the bottom left of the row with the needle coming up at 1. Take the needle diagonally over four threads to 2. Drop the needle vertically down behind four threads, bring it up at 3 and take it down at 4. Continue to create these diagonal bars along the row.

You will now return to the first diagonal stitch at the left of the row to create two loops in the petal colour. You can work each loop in the same colour, or each one in a different colour, or mix threads in the needle for a variegated shade.

Count four threads vertically directly above green 1 and bring the needle up at 1A. Take the needle over the green bar at its centre, then under the bar and back to 1A where the needle is taken down. Be very careful not to pull the loop too tight or you will distort the bar.

If you are working two different petal colours, work completely along the top row of the stitch first, taking the needle under four canvas threads horizontally to the right and coming up in the same hole at 2A. Create the loop and continue working the top loops along the row.

If you are working the same petal colour, complete each stitch as you go by taking the needle diagonally underneath four canvas threads to come up at 3A in the same hole as green 3. Take the needle over the bar and over the loop of the top stitch and back under the bar and the loop to 3A.

Above: Houndstooth stitch, shown here at centre, worked in attractive pink and purple threads.

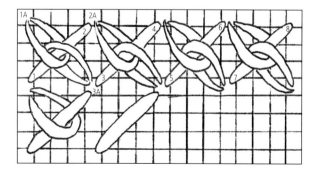
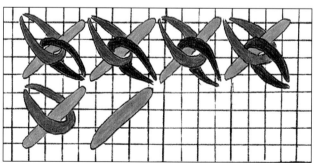

Right: Cross oblong double tied stitch, worked in a variety of seasonal colours, seen here at the centre of each picture.

Houndstooth variation stitch

This is worked exactly the same as houndstooth, except that this time you do pull the loops tight so that it looks like a stitch worked in a twisted thread. Once all your rows are in place, thread the needle with a colour using any type of thread except chenille. Now fill in the gaps between the stitches with straight rows of satin stitch squares. It can be very effective if you use a block of four or eight squares in one colour, and further blocks in other colours.

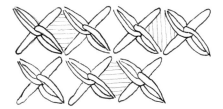

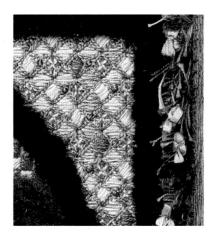

Above: Houndstooth variation stitch is an effective stitch for flowerbeds.

Cross oblong double tied stitch

This stitch is best worked using the larger crossed stitch as the green or other foliage colour and the two smaller parallel stitches as the flower colour. Once again, you can vary the colour by using different shades of thread in one needle.

To create the green stitch, thread up at 1 and down at 2, covering seven canvas threads diagonally. Leave one vertical row of canvas holes free. Drop the needle vertically behind seven canvas threads, come up at 3 and go down again at 4.

Place the small parallel stitches in the middle, just above and below the central cross. Work across two canvas threads up at A down at B; up at C down at D.

You will find it easier to place the structure of all the green foliage crosses first and then complete all the coloured parallel bars.

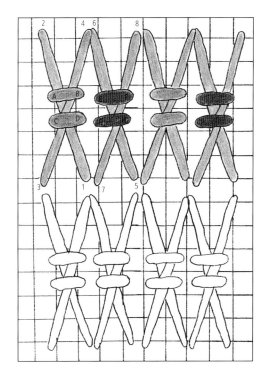

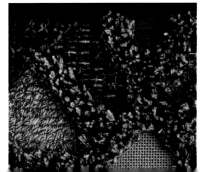

Flower stitch

Its name alone makes this an obvious choice to include in a flowerbed, and flower stitch is very effective as the coloured petals interlink with one another. For the best effect, blend the shades of petal colours together. For example, if you are working on a 24 count canvas, use six strands of stranded cotton in the needle in blending shades. The stitch is formed by working over four canvas threads creating narrow blocks that form a coloured flower cross. The foliage is worked in smaller blocks in between the petals.

Large flower cross

Starting on the lower side of the flower cross, bring the needle up at 1, take it over four canvas threads and down again at 2. Take the needle behind diagonally right to bring it up at 3 and vertically again to 4. Take the needle behind to the right over four canvas stitches and bring it up again at 5 and down at 6. Go behind diagonally again, up at 7 and down at 8. Continue in this way, following the sequence until the basic cross has been formed.

Small foliage cross

Create all the flower crosses first and then add the green foliage blocks between the petals. First work small back stitches over two canvas threads to form a square (see the diagram for the sequence). Then in the same foliage colour add a diagonal cross stitch in the centre worked in the usual way. Finally work a very small cross stitch in the centre of the petals, either in the petal colour, or in another colour to denote a stamen. The diagonal bars of the small cross stitches do not have to be uniform.

Above: Flowerstitch, worked here in blues and greens (top, centre) re-create the effect of hydrangeas (above).

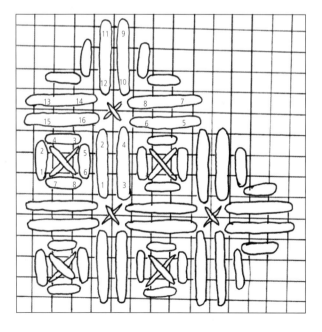

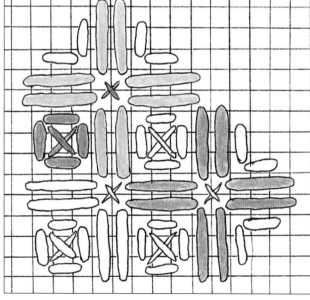

Rice stitch

Another simple stitch based on a cross, but less elongated than oblong double tied. The cross base should be worked in the green foliage colour and the colours inserted on the small stitch of each bar of the cross. Again, you will find it easier to work all the green structure first and then include the colours. You can try a variation of yarn, as well as colour. For example, wool for the base and stranded cotton or chenille for the small coloured bars. The stitch can also be embellished with beads.

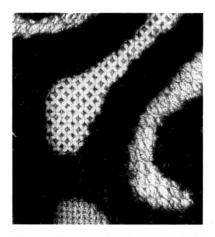

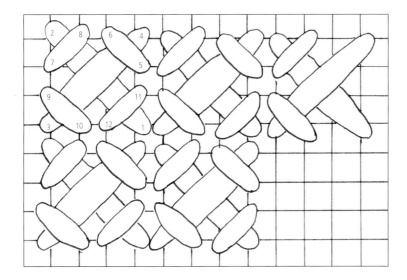

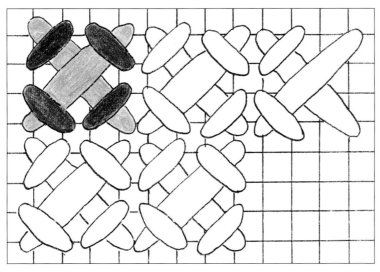

Above: Rice stitch, worked here in yellow (top), blue (centre), and red (bottom).

Cornered chain stitch

Work the vertical bars in green and the loops in colours. Experiment with the size of stitch you require for the appropriate flowerbed and place the green structure first by working up at 1, down at 2, up at 3 and down at 4. The loops lie proud of the canvas and are secured simply by slipping them through the thread of bar 3–4. To create the loops, which could be worked in fine ribbon, bring the needle up in the same hole at 2, take the needle diagonally down towards the green bar 3–4, and to secure it, pierce the bar from the right at the corner near 3, and take it under and back up to plunge down at 2. Take the needle across to 4 and repeat the process along the row.

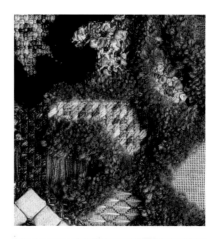

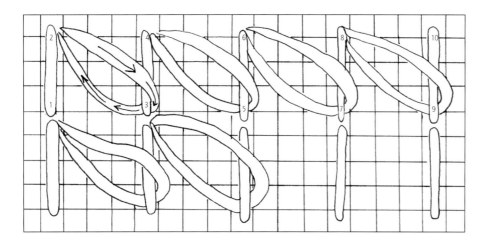

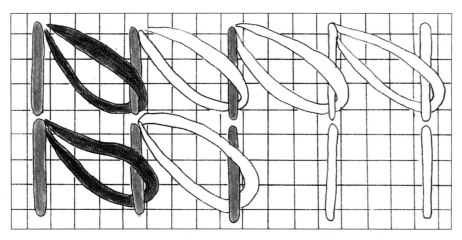

Right: Cornered chain stitch, at the centre of each picture, worked in a variety of seasonal colours.

Encroaching straight stitch

Placed vertically in a straight line, this stitch can be worked in the same colour to provide texture and interest in an area such as grass, earth or bedding plants. Work over eight canvas threads in a straight line from left to right, but once the first two stitches are in place drop to halfway down the second stitch to place the third and fourth stitches, then back up to the original level for the fifth and sixth stitches.

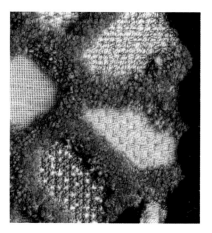

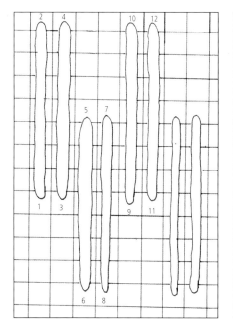

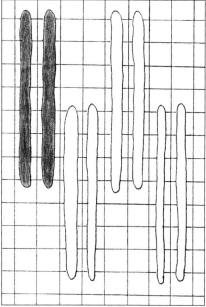

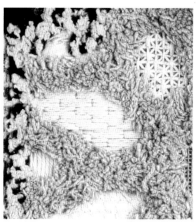

Right: Encroaching straight stitch, shown here at the centre of each picture in green, lilac, red and white, can be used to stitch grass, earth or flowerbeds.

Satin balloon stitch

Worked in horizontal rows, this attractive stitch expands and then contracts row by row to form a balloon shape. Work the stitch in one colour and then if you wish add a variation by placing three vertical fanned stitches on top of the balloon in a different colour.

Right: Satin balloon stitch worked here in green, with white fanned stitches over the top.

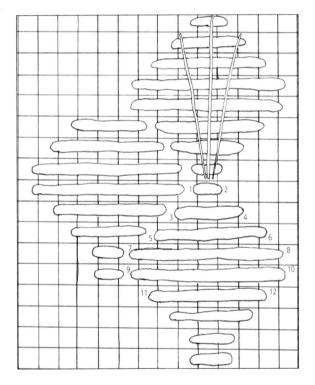

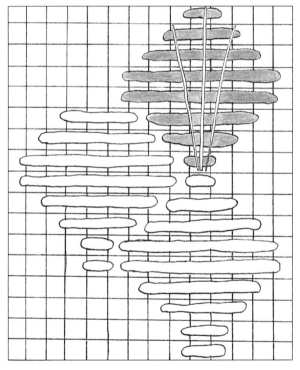

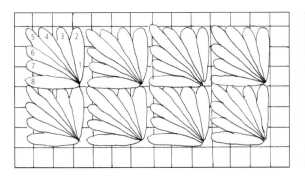

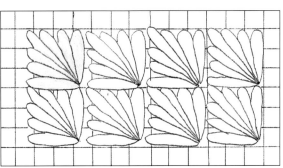

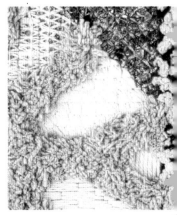

Fan or ray stitch

A very pretty stitch which can be worked in blocks of the same colour, or in variegated shades. Each rib of the stitch always comes up at 1 and radiates in a fan shape from 2 to 8. Always work in rows from left to right in a direction away from you, so start in the lower area first and work upwards. When you start second and subsequent rows, always begin in the canvas hole of point 2 of the stitch below.

Eyelet circular variation stitch

This creates a series of floral motifs with smaller flowers or foliage areas in between. The stitch radiates out from a central point to make sixteen petals. The petals do not have to be the same length – some can be shorter than others. Start at 1 and go down at 2, which is the central point of the flower. Repeat the process all around the flower.

Top: Fan stitch, centre, worked in white.

Above: Pinks, purples and blues are used to work an eyelet circular variation stitch.

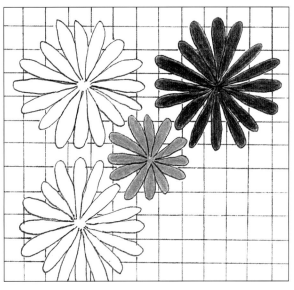

Bullion knots

A bullion knot can be an awkward little stitch, which sometimes does not take too kindly to sharing its space on the canvas. However, it is useful in a range of flowerbeds to add an extra dimension to the texture of the plants – and it's invaluable for representing slugs and snails if you are creating a realistic garden. A bullion knot combined with a tiny snail shell can be a charming feature. Except for chenille, any thread or wool can be used to form a bullion knot.

The length of the bullion knot will be dictated by you, so decide where it is going to fall on the canvas. It will start where you bring the needle up and finish at the point where the needle goes down through the canvas, but at first you will need to leave an amount of wool looped loosely between these two points so it can be curled around the needle to form the knot.

Make two small stab stitches to secure the thread and then take the needle to point 1 (A), where you want to start. Bring the needle up and then down at the required length of the stitch, 2 (B), leaving a loop of wool on the surface. Now take the needle back underneath to point 1 but push the point of the needle only through the canvas leaving the eye anchored at 2 (C). Wrap the looped wool on the surface clockwise around the shaft of the needle, keeping a slight tension on the wool so the loops lie side by side and do not fall over each other (D). If you find you have left too much wool on the surface, pull it gently underneath. Make sure that the coils are not too tight so that they can run up and down the shaft of the needle with ease.

Once you have coils to the required length of the knot, place your thumb and forefinger firmly over the coils on the needle. With the other hand pull the needle and gently ease it through the coils (E) Use the thumb and forefinger, pinching the coils, to place the knot correctly on the canvas as you pull the needle and wool completely through the coils (F) and then take the needle down again at point 2 to secure the stitch (G).

The main problem we have encountered with bullion knots is that stitchers get so stressed at the thought of making them that they try to keep control by wrapping the wool around the needle far too tightly. Consequently, there is no 'give' in the coils and the needle, including the eye, cannot slip through them. If the needle is pushed and shoved in an unseemly way, the coils will bunch up over each other and result in a mess, which can only be resolved by scissors and the complete removal of the knot.

However, the bullion knot is fun once you have mastered it. It is a creative stitch for the garden and a useful addition to any flowerbed, so relax and enjoy making some.

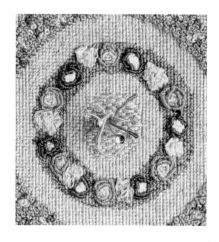

Above: Dainty bullion knots have been coiled around to create cabbages in a central feature.

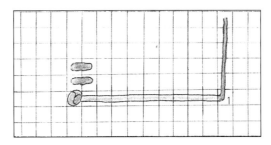

A

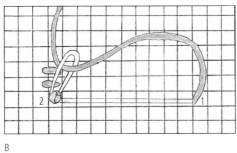

B

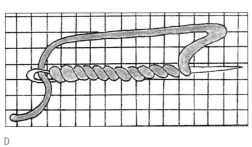

C

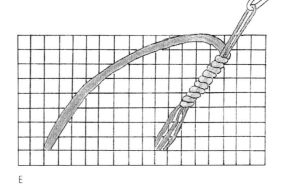

D

E

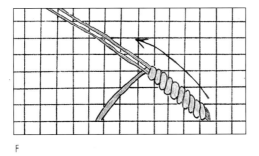

F

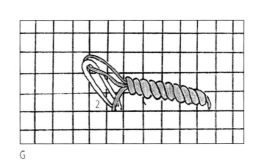

G

French knots

If you can make a bullion knot, a French knot will cause no problems at all. The French knot will sit on the diagonal of one canvas thread, like a tent stitch. The size of the stitch will be dictated by the number of threads you use in the needle. Bring the needle and thread up through the canvas at 1 in exactly the place you wish the knot to be (A). Wrap the wool near the canvas once anti-clockwise around the needle (B and C), angle the needle down towards the canvas keeping the tension on the thread with one hand and with the other plunge the needle down into the diagonally adjacent hole to secure the stitch (D and E). Bring the needle up in the hole next to the French knot and continue along the row. You can choose to work French knots in rows, or you can distribute them randomly where required. A pleasing effect is to speckle knots in different shades around the area or to blend different shades of stranded cotton in the same needle.

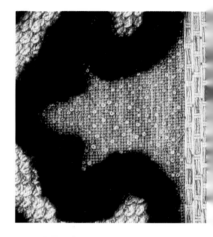

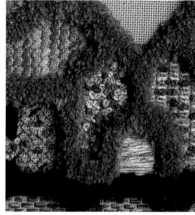

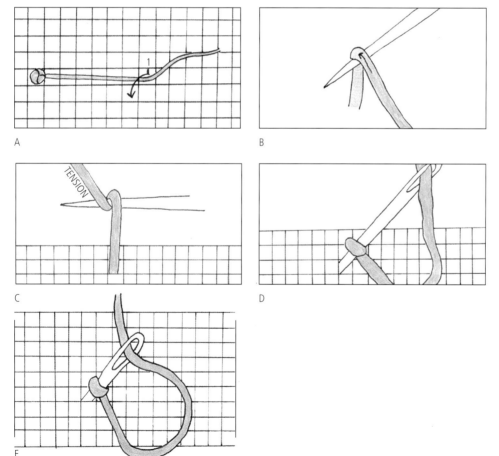

A

B

C

D

E

Above: Versatile French knots on flowerbeds and paths.

Other Techniques

Stumpwork – Woven Picot

With this fun and effective technique you can create 3-dimensional leaves or petals that grow upright out of the canvas base.

Method of working

The simplest way is to work the leaves in rows, starting with the nearest row to you and working away from you. Once you have gained more experience, you can work the leaves at different angles to each other in the flowerbed.

The picot is worked around a pin anchored into the canvas. If you are working on blank canvas, you can place the pin into the canvas and work directly over it. However, if you are working over existing stitches, place a piece of card over the area to avoid catching the needle in the stitches as you weave.

The length of the picot is determined by the placement of the pin in relation to the first stitch through the canvas. Before you start weaving, it's important to measure a long enough length of yarn to complete the whole leaf. It is possible to join the yarn halfway through the weaving process, but this is unnecessary if you prepare properly.

Bring the needle up at 1, which will be at the base of the leaf. Decide on the length of the leaf and anchor the pin where the tip of the leaf will be. Now take the thread up and around the pin, bringing it down two canvas threads to the right of 1 as at 2 in the diagram. Bring the needle up at 3, two threads to the right of 2, take the thread up and round the pin again so you now have three thread bars on which to weave. Starting at the top, weave underneath the first bar, over the middle one and under the third. Sharply pull the woven thread upward towards the pin to anchor the stitch tightly. Then continue from the top downwards weaving over and under the three bars, keeping the tension even and tapping the stitches up towards the pin at the top as you go. Make sure you do not pierce the bars and pull thread through them as you weave, otherwise you will not be able to tap the thread upwards and secure it.

As you travel down towards the base, the woven lines should be compact with no movement in the structure of the leaf. When you reach the base, plunge the needle down to the back of the canvas. At this stage you can tug on the thread below the canvas to distort the leaf if you wish. Remove the pin and manipulate the leaf into an upright position. Secure the picot underneath the canvas in the usual way. Pin the leaf forward so that it is kept out of the way while you work more.

You will need:

- A glass-headed pin
- A needle with an eye large enough to take your chosen thread
- Your choice of thread – stranded cotton, wool, ribbon, perlé
- A small piece of white card if you are working over an already stitched area

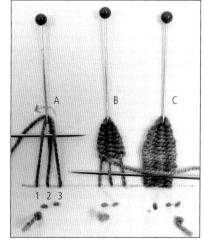

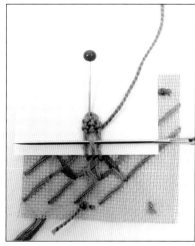

Needlelace leaves

Take an appropriate length of wire covered with stranded cotton (see page 66) and with a tail of cotton left at either end. Form a hooped leaf shape by bringing the two ends around to meet each other. Pinch together about 3mm (⅛in) at the ends of the wire. Thread the cotton tails through a needle and stitch the two ends of the wire securely together. This forms the base of the leaf (A).

Now take the needle through the wrapped thread again and pull it tight to create a secure stitch.

Take the needle up to the wire loop and insert it a few millimetres from the original stitch, pull the thread through gently and leave a loop on the inside of the hoop leaf (B).

Continue working around the outside of the leaf leaving loops – as if you were working a miniature blanket stitch – until all the frame has been covered (C).

To make the second row, use the first row of stitches as the base on which to secure the loops. As you have a decreasing space in which to work, you may find that you do not secure a new loop on every existing stitch.

Continue to create rows of loops until you can join them together in the centre. Now bring the needle down to the base of the leaf and make a few securing stitches (D). If you wish, manipulate the leaf to a different shape.

You can stitch the leaf directly on to the canvas, or you can thread the tail through a suitable bead to place the leaf in a planter before securing to the canvas. It is very effective to bring three or four leaves together and stitch them to a central covered wire, the top of which can be spiralled to represent a fresh young leaf about to open (see opposite).

Right: Attractive needlelace leaves add interest to the water feature in this embroidered knot garden.

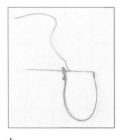

A

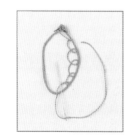

B

C

D

Ribbonwork – ribbon irises

Ribbon irises in contrasting shades look very realistic and give height and focus in the flowerbeds. They are great fun to make, if a little fiddly as you are working with short lengths of narrow ribbon, fine wire and one long strand of stranded cotton. At first you may feel that you are all fingers and thumbs – but continue practising and after you have made the first few you will find that your speed and accuracy increase. If you need a large number, you can enlist the help of family and friends and run a production line.

Method of working

Choose the shade of ribbon for the centre of the flower, and the shade you prefer for the lower petals or 'flags'. It is usual to use the lighter shade for the upper centre and the darker shade for the lower flags, but the choice is yours.

You will need:

- Fine gauge florist's wire or rice wire
- A wire cutter or old scissors
- A small pair of radio pliers with smooth jaws or strong, pointed tweezers
- Stranded cotton in varying shades of green, suitable for stems
- Two contrasting or complementary shades of ribbon, each 2mm (⅟₂in) wide
- Gutermann thread to match
- Fine chenille needle
- Fine embroidery needle (size 10 or 11)

Upper petals

Have ready a length of ribbon approximately 4–6cm (1½–2½in), depending on the size of flower head you require.

Cut a length of matching coloured Gutermann thread to approximately 17cm (7in). Tie a knot in one end and thread the other through an embroidery needle.

Now concertina the ribbon into 3 equal loops in a straight line. Pinch the two cut ends and the centre loop at the base together so that the loops at the top fan out (A).

Take your threaded needle and pass it through the pinched ends of the loops (B). Make a gathering stitch by taking the needle back and forwards two or three times through the ribbon to secure the loops. Remove the needle leaving approximately 15cm (6in) thread attached to the base of the ribbon loops.

A

B

Lower petals

As before, have ready a length of contrasting coloured ribbon approximately 4–6cm (1½–2½in). Cut a length of matching thread to approximately 17cm (7in). Tie a knot in one end and thread the other through an embroidery needle.

Again, concertina the ribbon into three loops, but this time bring the last loop round to an angle of 90 degrees to the other two (C). Take the threaded needle and make two or three gathering stitches to secure the loops at the base. When you remove the needle, again leave approximately 15cm (6in) of thread attached to the flower.

C

To complete the iris flower head

Plunge the thread of the upper petals through the centre of the lower petals (D). Position the upper petals gently onto the lower petals (E). Make sure at least one stitch goes down between each petal on the lower flower so that the iris will sit square on the stem (F). Leave both 15cm (6in) lengths of thread attached to the flower head as you will need them to secure the petals to the stem.

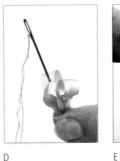

D

E

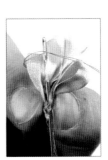

F

Covering wire to make the stems

Learning to spin one strand of stranded cotton around wire is a little like learning to spin wool from a traditional hand-held spindle. It takes a while to master the technique, but once you have done so, it is yours for life!

Rice wire comes already covered in paper and so it is tempting to buy green and use it straight away for the stems. However, you will find that covering the paper in twisted stranded cotton will give a much more professional finish. Also, if you use the same colour green paper throughout the garden for all stems, it will give an artificial look. Covering the stems in varying shades of green stranded cotton will result in a far more realistic garden.

Cut the wire to the required length for the stem, allowing about 5mm (¼in) extra at each end to secure the flower head and to anchor the stem into the canvas. Once you have spun the cotton onto it, you will be unable to cut the wire.

Cut a long length of one strand of stranded cotton. This must be enough to cover the entire length of the wire with a tight twist. Hold the wire and thread between your thumb and forefinger about 1cm (½in) from the end and wrap the thread clockwise towards the end of the wire (A).

When the thread reaches the end of the wire, use the pliers or tweezers to fold the wrapped end of the wire back on itself by approximately 3–5mm (⅛–¼in) to form a loop (B). Close the loop with one firm twist of thread. Continue to wrap the single strand of wire along its length by holding the loop of wire in your left hand and the cotton taut in your right hand. Roll the wire clockwise between the finger and thumb of your left hand and allow the cotton to twist up the wire to the end (C). Continue twisting clockwise with your left hand while your right hand holds the tension of the thread. As you work, use your right finger and thumb to 'bounce' the rolled cotton back up the wire against itself to create a smooth, taut, continuous coil.

If the tension slackens and then tightens again at any point, unravel the affected area and then continue along the wire as before.

When your tight cotton coil has reached the very end of the wire, take your pliers or tweezers again and bend the wire back on itself by approximately 3–5mm (⅛–¼in). There should still be enough stranded cotton attached to the end for you to thread through a fine needle and secure the coils of cotton on the folded end of the wire. Leave a length of cotton attached to enable you to secure the stem to the canvas.

A

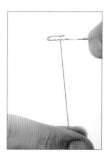

B

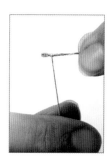

C

Attaching the flower heads to the stem

Take your pliers or tweezers and bend the hoop over at the top end of the stem so that it is at 90 degrees to the stem and forms a small circular platform, which will be parallel to the canvas base once the flower is finally in place (A).

Insert the base of the completed flower head gently into the circle of wire (B). Thread both strands of Gutermann thread you left attached onto a fine needle and secure the head onto the stranded cotton of the stem with a very small stitch.

Pull down one of the lower, darker colour flags of the iris head (C) so that it rests against the stem and secure with another tiny stitch (D).

Repeat this step twice again with the remaining darker petals (E and F).

Now you have mastered the art of making small ribbonwork flowers, you will find it easy to continue with more complex varieties and the techniques can be used again in making rambling roses. You can also use cotton-covered wires for a water feature.

A   B   C   D

E   F   G

Knitting

If you are a creative knitter, you can use this technique for small areas of grass, water or to represent earth. Using a plain garter stitch (A), stocking stitch (B) or moss stitch (C) and casting stitches on and off at the end of rows to fit the required shape, can create a very effective feature. Couch the completed knitted piece down with small stab stitches in the same coloured wool or thread (D).

Above: Moss stitch flowerbed with beaded flowers.

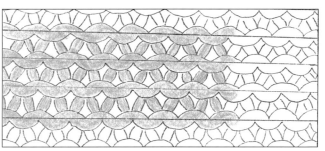

A Garter stitch

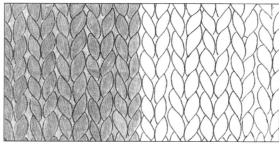

B Stocking stitch

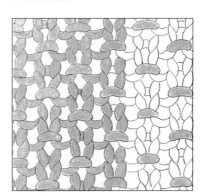

C Moss stitch

D

Historical background

What kind of plants would have been used in the flowerbeds? This really depends on the era in which you decide to set your garden. From the sixteenth century onwards as the explorers opened up trade routes to the East and the Americas the number of plants available to the wealthy increased dramatically decade by decade. Exotic new plants were much sought after not only as status symbols, but also to satisfy the growing interest in science and the natural world. Nurtured first by the gardeners of the wealthy in the great houses, the plants that thrived in the British climate would eventually filter out into general use.

However, even a very early Tudor garden would have had more choice and colour than you may think, including many herbs with their different coloured flowers.

The following herbs were among those known to be in use from the mid-fifteenth century onward: Betony, Borage, Chamomile, Clary sage, Coriander, Fennel, Hyssop, Rue, Rosemary, Sage, Savory, Tansy, Thyme and Wormwood. Other plants included: Agrimony, Bugle, Corn Marigold, Cornflower, Cowslip, Gillyflowers, Herb Robert, Hollyhock, Lavender, Mallow, Primrose, Pimpernel, Ragged Robin, Red Stocks, St John's Wort, Scabious, Teasel, Valerian, Violet and Viper's Bugloss.

The flowers contain a high proportion of shades of yellow and lavender, but some reds and blues as well. The foliage contains a wide range of shades of green from dark to almost silver.

5 Water features

No garden is complete without a spectacular water feature and you can have great fun experimenting with various methods of creating this vital focal point in your garden. The water feature should be inserted at the same time as you are stitching the flowerbeds. There are several ways to make a fountain, but bear in mind that any fountain or spouted water feature will need a foundation structure at its base to 'contain' the water. Any stitch may be used to form a base pond, but careful use of blended shades of blues, greens and greys in the needle can create a stunning overall effect. Depending on the type of garden, a pond or canal in a simple stitch will sometimes stand alone as a water feature.

When you make a fountain, it is important to include some of the shades that have been used in the base pond. It is a fairly straightforward procedure to construct a knotted jet fountain with thread. You can leave your 'water' spouting as a simple jet or, if you use longer lengths of thread, you can expand this into a more sophisticated fountain, with arcs of water returning to the base pond. Alternatively, you can either make a fountain with wire or combine the techniques of wire and thread for a more unusual feature.

Left: Fountains and water features provide a beautiful, and essential, focal point for any garden.

A knotted jet fountain

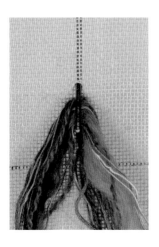

First, find a needle with a large eye. Bunch together a good length – at least 60cm (24in) – of a combination of several threads, each with a different texture, in toning watery shades. Knitting yarn, crewel wool, stranded cottons and chenille, for example, will all lie together in the same needle. Fit as many strands as you possibly can through the eye. Now pull the threads through the eye so that two even and equal lengths of about 30cm (12in) lie on either side of the needle (see illustration, left).

Plunge the needle down through the centre of the water feature, taking it through to the back of the work. Carefully pull your needle down, stopping while you still have a substantial amount of thread – about 13cm (5in) – left on the surface. Flip the frame over so the back of your canvas is in view. Take a pair of sharp scissors and cut right through the strands of thread at the centre by the needle. Take a group of released threads in each hand and tie a double knot resting on the back of the canvas. Be very careful not to pull your threads through from the front. Put your hand underneath and tug the threads from the front of the work to make sure the knot is tight on the back.

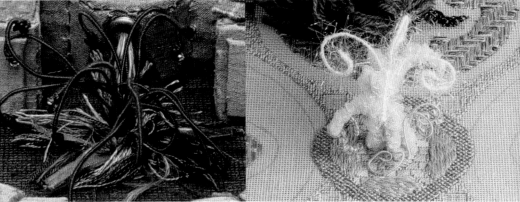
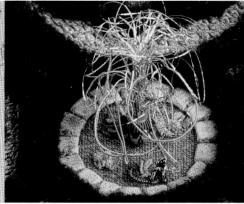

Still with your canvas wrong side up, divide the loose threads into four equal segments. Threading each segment through the needle in turn, plunge them through to the front at the four compass points – north, south, east and west – close to the centre knot. Turn the frame right way up and take a sharp pair of scissors. Holding the scissors straight down with the tip pointing directly at the canvas, carefully snip the bunched threads to shape a simple jet, with longer strands in the centre graduating to shorter lengths at the sides. Take great care that you do not cut through the base stitches on the canvas.

If you have left very long lengths of thread, you will, if you prefer, be able to create loops, stitching some or all of the threads back down through the canvas to create arcs of water. Secure the ends of the arcs to the canvas with stab stitches. This will expand your fountain from a simple jet to a more sophisticated water feature.

A wired fountain

This is based on the use of covered wires (see page 66). Wires can be covered in a range of toning water shades to match the pond. Alternatively, a fine lurex thread or space-dyed threads can be used. The wires could also be sprayed with paint and covered with a small amount of thread at the base to enable them to be stitched onto the canvas. To individualize the feature, small crystals or beads can be sewn to the wire to create light and sparkle.

Above: Covered wire, metallic thread, beads and glass can be combined to stunning effect in a range of water features.

Right: Use chandelier glass and beads for a traditional fountain.

Other ideas for water effects

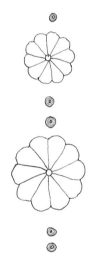

If you have ever been to Venice and succumbed to the temptation to purchase those sumptuous Murano glass beads, now is the time to use them for a ravishing effect. This feature is particularly pleasing in a square pond with a water jet in each corner.

Making sure first that the needle will fit through the centre of your bead, thread about 15cm (6in) each of as many mixed threads in water tones as will fit onto a large-eyed needle. Tie a single knot at the end of the threads and bring the needle up from behind the canvas at the centre of the water feature until the knot sits firmly underneath the canvas. Holding the threads taut above the work, take the bead through the needle and force it down over the threads until it sits firmly on the canvas. Now take a pair of sharp scissors and cut the threads to the height and shape of your desired jet of water. The cut threads will cascade back over the bead, forming a delightful feature with light reflected from the glass container bead.

Small segments of chandelier glass, set on other beads, can also be used to create water effects. Take some small, flat beads, preferably in greeny-blue shades (beads with a mother-of-pearl effect are perfect for this feature). Thread a needle up through the centre of a bead and then thread through the chandelier glass so that it sits horizontally on top of the bead. If you wish, you can thread a smaller piece of glass on top of the first and finish off with more beads (as shown left).

Flakes of mica can be secured on top of a stitched base to create reflections for any water feature.

Shisha mirror glass can be used for a simple square pond. Divide the square into four triangles and then stitch from the edge of the square towards the centre, using laid stitches, which you can stagger, as in a split stitch, to introduce more shades. Again, you can blend different shades in the needle if you wish (A).

To secure a mirror, take one thread from the mix and sew it down over the mirror, in the direction of the base stitch following the numbered stitch sequence (B).

Any other artefact that reflects light and sparkles – crystals, sequins or semi-precious stones – can be sewn onto a stitched base.

A very exciting representation of water can be made by using metallic fabric. Boil the fabric for approximately two minutes, after which it will shrink and crinkle dramatically. Shards of the fabric can then be cut and twisted, rolled and manipulated into watery shapes (C). Choose a Gutermann thread of the same colour as the fabric to secure the shapes, bearing in mind that everything must radiate from the centre of the water feature.

Above, from left: Shisha mirrors, machine embroidery and a jacquard canvas stitch make interesting water features.

Right: A natural pond using a mirror covered with embroidered gauze.

A

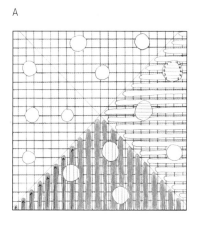

B

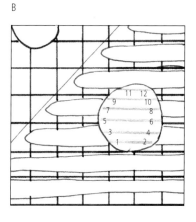

C

Left: Added features such as fish
and plants can be easily represented.

Right: Metal fabrics can be
cut and manipulated to cover
ready-made structures.

You can devise ways of personalizing a water feature and adding interest quite simply:
for example, fish can be represented with use of a stitch in orange wool or stranded
cotton, or a gold or rainbow thread. If your garden is to be less than perfect, you could
choose to have some green algae 'growing' in a corner of the pond with the use of
French knots. Tiny real pebbles could be introduced, as could small models of frogs
or toads, available from dolls' house suppliers.

To make the spectacular fantasy-land feature, illustrated opposite, you have the
following choices: either go to evening classes and learn how to weld, so you can make
your own metal framework, or buy a small metal Christmas tree at the appropriate
time of year and cut it to a the correct size and shape with a pair of wire cutters.

Historical background

Water has always been a welcome presence in man-made gardens, and complex and
sophisticated water features have been status symbols in gardens for longer than you
may think. If you are re-creating a 17th-century garden and think that a flamboyant
water feature would be out of place, you may be surprised to know that as early as
1608 the Huguenot engineer and designer Salamon de Caus was working for James I
and his Queen, Anne of Denmark. De Caus's extraordinary water features, grottoes
and automatons at Somerset House and Richmond Palace were renowned. Later in the
century, his younger brother Isaac continued the tradition, working with the architect
Inigo Jones to create ambitious feats of hydraulic engineering in spectacular gardens.
Unfortunately, no known examples of the de Caus brothers' work survive today.

6 Hedging and topiary

Left: The hedges in this colourful garden add to the seasonal effect.

Once all paths, flowerbeds and water features are complete, the final stitchery on the garden itself is to form the hedging. As in a real garden, the hedge will encroach over the edges of paths and flowerbeds, so these need to be in place first in order that you can make your final trim of the hedge to fit the effect you require in the borders. Walls, especially those that include climbing plants, are a beautiful but time-consuming addition, and can be worked after the rest of the garden is finished.

Anyone thinking of a knot garden anticipates beautifully trimmed hedges forming intricate patterns. Hedges are the core of the garden and shape its essential personality. At the design stage, you will have put a lot of thought into choosing colours and shapes that will affect the whole mood of your garden. At this stage, and again just before you start to trim, you will find it useful to refer to your original line drawing to check on the exact placing of your hedging. Once you have worked the plushwork stitch for the hedge, and before you cut, it may be difficult to see the garden properly, as it will be obscured by the hedging wool.

It is important to choose the correct wool to turn your ideas into reality, since the type of thread you use is crucial to the overall final appearance of the hedge. A plushwork stitch will appear the same, whatever count of canvas it is worked on – it is the yarn you choose that will affect the basic appearance of the hedge. Plushwork worked on a 24-count canvas will ultimately appear slightly more compact than that worked on a 10-count, but the overall appearance of the stitch remains the same.

There are three different types of wool suitable for the purpose, and your choice will depend on the desired effect.

1) Crewel wool is superb for a fine clipped low box hedge, especially one that is no wider than about 2cm (¾in).

2) Tapestry wool is suitable for chunkier hedging, especially if it is to be seen growing up a brick wall.

3) Knitting yarn allows for creative experiments and a totally free approach to technique: for example, in the winter segment of the seasonal knot garden (see page 78) a tweeded yarn is used to create a snow-covered hedge, while small glass beads or judicious use of glue can be used to give the effect of hoar frost.

Above: Flowerbeds in place before the plushwork is stitched.

Below: The completed hedge will encroach over the edges of the paths and flowerbeds.

Above: A small matchbox container adapted to create a courtyard garden using 24-count canvas.

Another approach is to use a combination of all these threads to create a mixed hedge. Use a 'host' thread, such as crewel, with a speciality yarn running through it. So, for example, mohair, strands of stranded cotton in a mixture of colours, or perlé could be used with the host to give the hedge a variety of textures and colours. With a careful selection of colours you can create a lavender hedge, a deep blue ceanothus growing up a brick wall or a copper beech hedge.

If you are working a hedge for the first time, you may feel more secure using one type and shade of wool, but be prepared to be adventurous and experiment with different effects. Remember that you have your sampler on which to try out different combinations of wool and to see how they trim down to a finished hedge before you commit yourself to the final choice.

The best stitch to use for hedging is plushwork. Although this is a very wasteful stitch, using vast quantities of wool, it is very effective and no knot garden is complete without it. As the stitch is very dense, be aware that the colour you choose will appear much darker once it is stitched and cut. Even if you want a dark hedge, we suggest you use wool a few shades lighter in tone than your intended finished colour, as you will find that the final result appears darker than you expect.

If in doubt, measure out a 2.5cm (1in) square on your sample canvas and stitch it in plushwork to gauge the finished colour. This exercise will also help you to calculate the quantity of wool you will need for the final project.

It is best to buy your wool from a source that is unlikely to discontinue the supply. Even so, try to over-estimate the amount you will need so you can buy a good quantity of a shade from within the same dye-lot. It is surprising how dramatic variations of colour in different dye-lots of the same shade can be, and we have experienced a variety of emotions among embroiderers, ranging from deep disappointment to hysterical tantrums, when they have run out of a chosen colour which cannot subsequently be exactly matched.

Simple plushwork

Cut a length of wool that is manageable for sewing. If you are using a mix of colours, choose a needle large enough to take all the wools and threads together. Thread your needle and start on the first row.

Plushwork is worked in a straight line from left to right, and the first row of stitches will be the row nearest to you. The next row of stitches above that will be further away from you. As you work, always leave a clear path of canvas above and gently flatten the loops you have already made towards you. This allows you to stitch new loops easily without trapping the ones you have already made. As you work, the rows of loops will fit together with the appearance of tiles or feathers.

You will need:

- Any count of canvas
- Pointed needle with eye to fit the chosen wools
- Chosen wools/threads

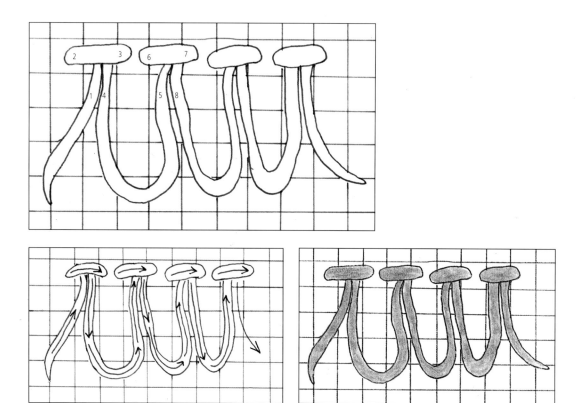

A plushwork anchor stitch

Leave one canvas hole free at the left-hand edge of the first row and, working from
above, take your needle down through the second hole along at 1. Pull the thread
down through the canvas, carefully leaving a tail of about 5cm (2in) of wool above.

Hold onto the wool tail above and move the needle, which is underneath the canvas, to
the hole to the left of the original insertion point. Bring the needle up at 2, pulling the
thread all the way through the canvas while ensuring that you hold onto the tail tightly.
Pass the needle to the right, taking it over two canvas threads so that you enter the
hole to the right of the tail at 3. Pull the thread firmly all the way down through the
canvas. Now angle the needle to the left and bring it up through the centre hole that
contains the tail, 4.

To create loops

Having come up through the same hole as the tail, take the needle over two canvas
threads to the right and plunge it down through the hole at 5. Leave a loop of thread
above the surface so that the top of the loop is about 2cm (1in) taller than you wish
your hedge to be. Bring the needle up to the left again through the hole containing the
original anchor stitch at 6. Take the needle over two more canvas threads to the right to

create another anchor stitch. Take the needle down at 7 and bring it up at 8 which shares the same hole as 5.

Continue with this stitch, which is, in effect, a backstitch leaving loops, until you reach the end of the row. Finish by bringing the final thread back up to the top and cutting it off, leaving a tail.

While working the row, you may find it useful to hold a pencil or a lollypop stick at the required height and parallel to the canvas as a guide to help you to keep the loops even.

If you are using a very fine count of canvas, you may find when you come to work second or subsequent rows that the thickness of the wool has pushed the canvas threads out of place. If this has happened, leave the distorted row and work along the next clear row of canvas.

It is important to work whole rows completely from left to right. If the hedge is in any form of shape that curves around to meet itself, you should work both sides of the circle or swirl contemporaneously. The stitching should always be kept level at both sides of the shape and the path ahead of the whole shape must always be clear. If you try to work continuously around a swirl, the loops will be above you on the return journey and will get trapped as you stitch, unless you turn the entire frame around as you work.

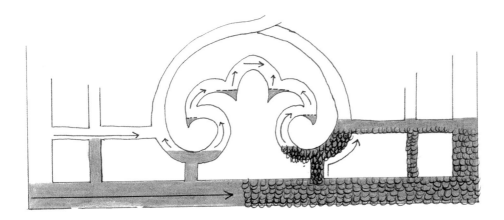

Left: The arrows on the diagram show the direction of the stitch.

Trimming the hedges

This process requires great care and real courage, but if you have stitched the plushwork correctly, it will not fall out when you cut it unless you inadvertently cut through the anchoring stitches. Even if you do cut through the anchoring stitches, or if you accidentally cut a path or flowerbed, everything at this stage is retrievable. Pull out the cut area, sew any loose ends into the back of the work to secure them, and re-stitch the area.

You must have a pair of very sharp embroidery scissors with a blade of a size that is manageable in your hand. Pinking shears or kitchen scissors just will not do! Always be very careful when positioning the scissors for a cut, as it is very easy to cut the canvas unintentionally. If you do cut the canvas unintentionally, you can make a repair with buttonhole thread, which is a similar weight to canvas thread. Secure the buttonhole thread with a small double stitch under a stitched area of canvas, then take it over the cut area and anchor the other end below your stitches. Introduce the warp threads first and then weave the weft threads through them. Once you have a grid in place again, continue stitching the garden.

Right: A large quantity of wool is lost during clipping.

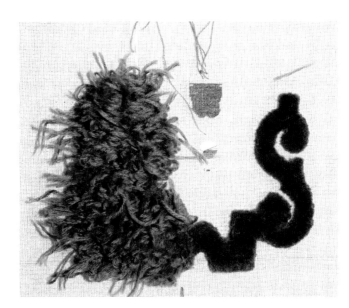

Above: Plushwork showing combined yarns – mohair and knitting wool.

If you are right-handed, it is a good idea to start as near as possible to the bottom left-hand side of the canvas, this being the easiest area to handle. If you are left handed, start in the opposite corner. However, do not start where the hedging is forming a knot, curve or circle, but with the simplest part of the design: select a straight line and work a trial area first to gauge the finished height of the hedge and to form a guide for the rest of the garden. Although you will eventually find that you cut back a lot of wool, start with a modest amount at first and gradually reduce the size of the hedge with subsequent trimmings. Remember that you cannot replace the wool once it is cut!

Before you start to cut, refer again to your line drawing to remind yourself of the intended width of the final hedge. If the hedge is to be narrow (say over five threads of canvas), you can afford to cut away more severely at first – a narrow hedge should ultimately be short and well clipped back or it will look out of proportion and start to droop. If the hedge is wider, you should be more circumspect as to the amount of wool you remove at the first cut.

When you are satisfied with the size of the guide hedge and are confident with cutting, you can trim the rest of the hedging. You might make one cut each for the top and sides, or you can continue to cut overall, cutting gradually and in layers until you have reached the guide size. As you trim, either remove the cut wool with sticky tape or frequently turn the frame upside down and give it a sharp tap to dislodge the cut wool, allowing it to fall away.

Place the blades of your scissors so that they are parallel to the canvas and flat across the top of the plushwork and cut flat, as if you were trimming a real hedge. Use the whole length of the blades so that they cut smoothly across the top of the loops.

Once you have achieved the required height for the first cut on the top of the hedge, turn your scissors and, using the same technique of cutting with the entire length of the blades, very carefully make the second cut along the side of the hedge that faces the outside of the garden. Start at the top of the hedge and work downwards, cutting

Above: An aerial view of twist
and tension knotted hedging.

at an angle of about 45 degrees so that the hedge is narrower at the top and wider at
the bottom. Leave the very bottom layer of loops uncut until you are completely
satisfied with the final size of the hedge. When you are happy with the size, cut the
bottom loops away extremely carefully, cutting around the bottom of the hedge so that
approximately 2mm (¹⁄₁₂in) of hedge covers the adjoining border of path or flowerbed.

Make the third cut in a similar manner, cutting along the side of the hedge that faces
into the garden.

Shaping a complicated knot

For a hedge that is to look as if it is twisting and turning under and over itself with a
sense of movement, you will need to take even more care with the cutting process.
First of all, trim the hedge as described above until you can clearly see the outline of
the final shape and width. This done, return once again to the original line drawing
and very carefully check which areas should appear to run under and which run over.
If necessary, pin labels to the hedge to indicate where you should cut away so that the
hedge will gradually dip down, giving the illusion of running under. Using the point of
the scissors, clip away to create a gradual gradient of hedge sweeping down towards
the hedge that is to run over. At the other side of the top hedge, cut down to the same
level you left on the original side and then pick up the same gradient to sweep back up
to the highest point you require.

Historical background

What types of plant were used for hedging? We tend to think of box as the obvious plant for hedging knot gardens today, but there is no evidence that this was much used in the Tudor period. Contemporary accounts refer to herbs such as hyssop, lavender, marjoram, myrtle, rosemary, rue, southernwood and thyme.

There is some evidence that box was used in the gardens of Roman villas and it may have been introduced to Britain from Italy at some point during the Roman occupation. However, box seems to have fallen out of favour in England until about 1600, when it was gradually re-introduced as a hedging and topiary plant.

Above: A beautifully sculpted garden using a lighter yarn for simple pompons.

Topiary

The most amazing topiary effects can be achieved with the imaginative use of simple pompons. Everyone remembers making pompons as a child, and this is another good opportunity to get children, friends and family involved in your project by setting up a pompon production line.

Tapestry wool in the same shade as the hedge is the best choice for topiary trees, as it is thick and therefore fills up the void of the pompon maker quickly, compacting into a tight area. However, if you have used mixed yarns for the hedging and wish to preserve a uniform effect, you can use the same combination for the trees.

There are various forms of pompon maker on the market and one of the most simple consists of three sizes of plastic disc, allowing you to adjust the size and density of each pompon. For the best results for an embroidered knot garden of the average size, you would probably use the small or medium gauge.

Alternatively, you can cut your own discs out of cardboard to exactly the size you want using a compass to help you draw them up first.

You will need

- Tapestry wool
- Strong linen thread/ buttonhole thread in a dark colour
- Yarn darner
- A pompon maker, either bought or cut from cardboard

Above: Topiary shapes, like these from Great Dixter, East Sussex, can inspire embroiderers to experiment with different techniques.

The diameter of the discs should be slightly bigger than the size of your intended pompon, as this will allow you scope to trim it. In the centre of each disc, there should be a void, which will fill with wool as you gradually wrap it around. If you are using cardboard, cut one disc as a template first and use it to cut the discs for all the pompons you intend to make of the same size. This will ensure that the pompons will be of a standard size.

Take two identical discs and place one on top of the other. Thread a yarn darner with tapestry wool and slide the needle between the two discs, pulling the wool into the centre and leaving a tail on the outside. Pinch the discs where the wool passes between them and then wind the wool in a clockwise direction around both layers of disc. Continue winding until the void in the centre is filled with wool. Using a yarn darner will enable you to pull the wool through easily as it starts to compact in the void.

Have a strong linen buttonhole thread to hand and a pair of sharp scissors. Carefully insert the point of the scissors between the outer edge of the two layers of card and, turning the discs as you go, cut around the wool loops at the circumference. The strong linen thread will be used not only to secure the wool of the pompon, but also to stitch it into place in the garden, so be sure to cut a long length. Insert the thread horizontally between the two discs, pull it tight and tie a double knot, leaving a good (double) tail. Next, gently slip the cardboard discs off to reveal your pompon and trim it gently and evenly to the required size.

Securing the trees to the canvas

The simplest tree is represented by a single pompon attached to the canvas in the appropriate place.

Thread both tails of the linen thread through the needle and plunge it down through the canvas. Pull the thread tight from underneath so that the pompon rests on the canvas. Once you are satisfied that the tree is correctly placed in the garden, turn the frame over, pull one strand of the linen thread tail out of the needle and zigzag the tail left in the needle though the other stitches on the back of the canvas. Then thread the other tail and zigzag it through stitches in the opposite direction. This spreads out the anchoring of the pompon like the roots of a tree, and avoids leaving a lump of securing stitches underneath.

To make a taller, tiered tree, take three pompons of staggered size – small, medium and large. Thread the two linen tails of the smallest pompon through the yarn darner. Take the medium-sized pompon and, holding it so the linen tails hang down, plunge the point of the darner directly through the centre, so that the needle exits where the medium tails hang. This will leave four strands of linen thread hanging together and two pompons fitting snugly one on top of the other. Thread the four strands onto the darner and repeat the process with the largest pompon so that you have six strands of linen thread hanging at the bottom and three pompons joined to each other to make a tree (as shown left).

Place the tree in the required place in the garden, thread all six tails together and plunge them through the canvas as with the single pompon. Turn the frame over and zigzag each tail end through the stitches at the back so that they run in different directions and are evenly spread out, again without leaving a lump.

Trees can also be put into pots. Look for a supplier of dolls' house equipment to find pots that will be in proportion to the size of your garden. If possible, use little terracotta pots of the type with a hole in the bottom, so that you can pass the securing tail threads through to attach the pot to the canvas. Otherwise, you will carefully have to make your own opening on the base of the pot with a small craft ceramic drill.

If you are going to put your trees into pots, ensure that you have extra long tails on the pompons so that your thread will pass through all the pompons, plus the pot, and still leave enough length to secure the pot to the canvas, using the zigzag method.

Left: A simple circular hedge draws the eye towards the central feature. Pompon trees in different coloured wools add interest to the trees.

Above: A three-tiered pompon with securing yarn.

Historical background

If it appeals to you, do not be afraid of introducing extravagant topiary into your garden. Topiary is not a modern enthusiasm – the Romans enjoyed fantastic creations formed out of box and there are contemporary accounts from the Tudor period of fabulous beasts fashioned from plants and herbs growing on willow structures.

One of the best gardens to visit for inspirational topiary is Levens Hall in Cumbria, England. Through a quirk of history, Levens avoided the 'improvements' of the Landscape Movement of the 18th century and the original yews, planted in the 1690s as part of a formal parterre garden, survive today. During the late 18th and 19th centuries, the yews began to be fashioned into the fantastical 'Wonderland' shapes in which they are kept today. The topiary garden at Levens will enthral anyone with an eye for shape, texture and the play of light on natural surfaces.

Below left: Topiary in Levens Hall Gardens, Cumbria.

Below right: The Privy Garden at Hampton Court Palace, Surrey.

7 Brick walls

The final project will be the building of brick walls. Walls are not essential to the knot garden, but the representation of an ancient, mellow wall basking in sunlight and reflecting a palette of subtle colours can change the mood of the garden and enhance its personality. However, be warned that creating them is a 'tour de force' and has to be a labour of love involving untold hours of stitching.

Our original garden was based on a 17th-century design, but the wall was inspired by the Tudor brickwork surrounding the rose garden at Hampton Court Palace. Your first step is to decide on the type of wall you require for your garden – a 16th- or 17th-century structure of hand-made bricks, a Victorian wall with machine-made bricks or, depending on the style of your garden, a contemporary wall made with modern materials, such as steel, plastics or glass tiles.

If you decide to re-create a traditional wall, it is essential to spend some time looking closely at brick structures. This will cause great amusement among your family and friends, but do not be deterred. The history of brickwork and the study of walls can be absolutely fascinating, especially when you propose to re-create a wall in thread.

Sketch the areas of the wall you decide to reproduce and, if possible, take photographs at different times of day. You will notice that if the wall is constantly exposed to sunlight in one particular area, the colours will be bleached lighter at that point. Also, one side of the wall may be much darker and damper than the other, depending on the orientation of the wall to the sun, and you may wish to reproduce this phenomenon in your own garden. Obviously, morning, midday and evening sun will not only fall in different areas, but each will also have a completely individual light quality. This will affect the mood of the wall and ultimately the entire garden, so decide at which time of day you intend to set your scene and choose the colours accordingly.

Left and right: Each brick has its own shade and texture – an exciting challenge for an embroiderer

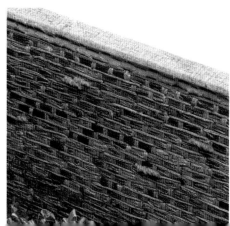

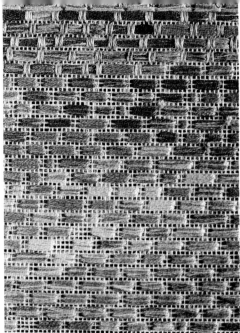

Above: Use blended shades of green to interpret moss and algae at the base of the wall.

Look carefully at the colours in the brickwork – you will be surprised at how many you will find. If you can, take an embroidery shade card with you and match up the colours you see. The wall will not only be faded in different areas according to where the sun falls on it, but will change colour with the condition of the bricks. You will find that bricks at the bottom of the wall are relatively dark and green from coverings of moss and algae (see above, right); as you progress up the wall, the brick colourings emerge and the mortar becomes whiter.

Become aware of the size, shape and texture of the bricks. A wall that is several hundred years old will be of hand-made bricks that are smaller than modern day ones and of uneven size and irregular, roughened appearance. Some lesser-worn bricks will appear 'fatter' than others; you can represent this by stitching certain bricks with more strands of cotton in the needle. The original design of some walls includes patterns made by juxtaposing bricks either of different colours or of different sizes. Sometimes, these are faded and hard to discern and it can be very exciting if, after studying a wall for some time, you become aware of the ghost of the original design still visible in the brickwork. At Hampton Court, the dark diaper patterns (see below) are still very obvious and these have been re-created in our original knot garden.

Below and left: Incorporating a diaper pattern into your embroidered wall will add detail and interest.

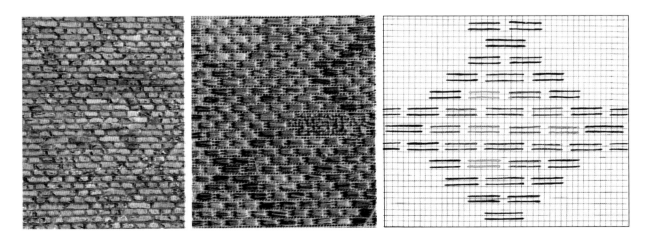

Man-made forms, such as buttresses and top dressing stones, can add interest. Don't forget the inevitable large nails in the wall – or the holes they have left in the bricks – showing where generations of gardeners over the centuries have provided support for their precious plants. Then there are the natural features – climbing plants and wildlife. Wall shrubs and creepers provide a haven for birds, insects and small mammals, such as hedgehogs, and these can all be represented in your garden.

Decide which plants you wish to reproduce and then very carefully study the way they grow against the wall. The original stem of an old rose, for example, may be established a fair distance from the present blooming foliage and flowers, so you can make its long stem run across the wall. Shrubs that grow against a wall may either have been clipped to an artificial shape or allowed to develop freely so that they bush out quite noticeably at the top. Remember that by working a bush in a darker shade at the bottom, you can re-create an illusion of shadow.

The planting on the walls can be of all kinds, shapes and sizes. You may wish to incorporate fanned fruit trees – apricots, apples, pears or even figs and, depending on the season of your garden, these may be full of blossom or heavy with fruit. In a summer garden, you can reproduce roses, honeysuckle, clematis and wisteria. If you want to highlight your garden as a place of peace, order and sanctuary, it makes a very effective contrast if the plants inside the garden are formally trained and clipped, while those on the outside walls are allowed to grow wild and unkempt.

Above: Natural features such as crumbling brickwork and weeds can add interest to embroidered walls.

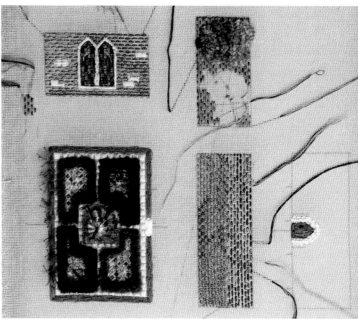

Planning the wall

Walls should be worked only on either a 22- or a 24-count canvas.

First decide on the height of your walls, which should be in pleasant proportion to the garden. Four two-sided brick walls will require a lot of stitching so do not be tempted to make them too high. Draw a plan of each of the eight walls to size, positioning the buttresses on one side if you are including them. If you wish to display a diaper pattern, carefully measure the walls and mark the pattern to size on the design.

Next, plan where the plants will be on each side and what shape they will take.

You will draw the shape of trees, bushes and shrubs onto the canvas and then work the brickwork stitches up to the edges of these outlines. Do not stitch areas of wall that will lie underneath plushwork plants; this will pointlessly add to your time, as the stitches will never be seen once the plants are in place.

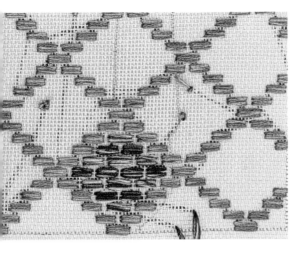

Trees can also be formed with a mixture of chunky chenille thread for the foliage and raised band stitch for the trunk (see instructions on page 104) and space can be left on the canvas for this technique to be worked. Rambling plants with thin stems, however, such as roses, will be couched directly onto the stitched bricks.

Once you are satisfied with your design, draw and trace the design as you did with the original garden plan and then transfer it to canvas (See pages 25–26). It is worth spending some time putting a palette of colours together. First, look at all the shades of stranded cotton and divide them into appropriate colours for each stage of the wall, from top to bottom. Have a card for each stage with six holes punched into it. Cut a short, manageable length off each skein of stranded cotton and then separate the strands. Some bricks you will wish to make all the same colour, but for most of them mix the strands into different proportions of colour combinations – for example 1:5, 2:4, 3:3 or 2:2:1:1. When your cards are prepared, place your mixed stranded lengths through the holes so they are easy to handle as you stitch and you can see at a glance the colour combination you have to hand. In general, you would use 6 strands of cotton in the needle unless you wish to make the occasional 'fatter' brick, in which case you should add two to four more strands.

As a guide to starting the darker, bottom bricks we suggest two strands of green, two strands of brown, one strand of light red and one strand of cream.

Above: Brick patterns in walls symbolized wealth and extravagance in England in the 16th and 17th centuries.

Right: Work bricks first and add plant features later.

Left: A fabric wall stamped with suitable paint on fabric and embellished with French knots makes a good alternative to stitched bricks.

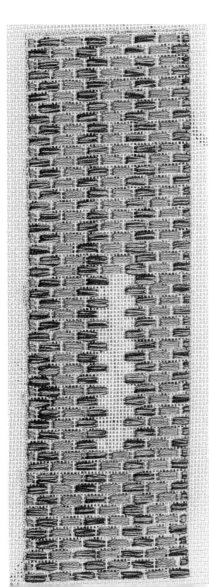

For an aesthetically pleasing and realistic effect, do not work complete horizontal rows of the same colour combination. Work, say, six to eight bricks in the same colour combination and then change to a slightly different combination, creating a subtle speckling of colour horizontally along the wall as well as obvious changes on the vertical.

For a realistic representation of a tree trunk, leave a space between bricks to couch down driftwood at its centre. Cover the couching stitches with stumpwork leaves and ribbon flowers (see photos, left).

The brickwork stitch

We recommend that working horizontally you cover six canvas threads at a time with stranded cotton, but be sure to work an area of brickwork on your sampler first in order to check that you have a satisfactory size of brick in relation to the size of your wall. Working a sample first will also give you some idea of how long the entire wall will take to stitch.

Bring the needle up at 1 and take it horizontally to the right over six threads of canvas; bring the needle down at 2 and pull it through so that the stranded cotton sits tight on the top of the canvas. Go back to 3, which is the canvas hole immediately below 1; pull from below then again take the needle horizontally to the right and plunge down into 4, which is immediately below 2. This completes the first brick and could be likened to the first step of a journey of a thousand miles. One vertical thread of canvas will be left bare between each horizontal brick.

You will need:

- 22- or 24-count canvas
- 12 or more shades of stranded cotton, chosen to fit your wall's colour scheme
- A sharp-pointed needle with an eye big enough to take six or more strands of cotton

Above: Diagram for working a diaper pattern.

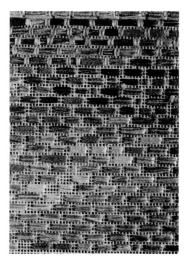

TOP
Weathered
Mixed brick colours

MID
Mixed bleached/red/orange

UPPER BASE
Damp brick
Green and red/ orange / brown
Off green

BASE
Green

The mortar stitch

Once you have removed the cotton from the natural tea/coffee dye, either leave it out flat in the sun to let it dry or use a hair dryer. Do not on any account put it in the tumble dryer – even if it is wrapped in fabric for the purpose it will emerge like a knotted bird's nest. If you are really brave, take the dyed thread into the garden and stain it by rubbing it in soil or moss, but do make sure it has completely dried out again before you start to stitch.

Vertical mortar

It is important to fill in the vertical lines of mortar first so that the start and finish of these stitches will eventually be disguised by the horizontal mortar.

Begin at the top of the wall and work downwards on the vertical lines. Find the canvas thread exposed between two bricks. Thread four strands of cotton onto the needle and bring it up from underneath, in the hole directly above the top right-hand corner of the brick and to the left of the exposed canvas thread, 1. Take the needle down in a straight line over three canvas threads to the exposed hole between the rows, 2. Bring the needle back up to the right of the vertical canvas thread and next to where the stitch started, 3. Take it back down to the space below the brick at 4.

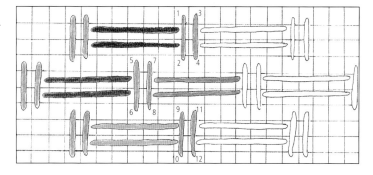

Now move the needle left and down to the canvas thread between the lower bricks and repeat the process 5 to 8. Continue in this manner down to the bottom of the wall infilling the vertical mortar.

Horizontal mortar

Again using 4 strands to the needle, work a simple split stitch across the row. Bring your needle up in the first canvas hole of the row and take it to the right over any number of threads of canvas up to a maximum of 17. Plunge the needle down, take it back to the left to the centre of the stitch and bring it up and move again to the right on top of the canvas. The stitches do not have to be of uniform length along the row but make sure that the stranded cotton covers the top and bottom stitches of the vertical mortar and does not share the same canvas hole.

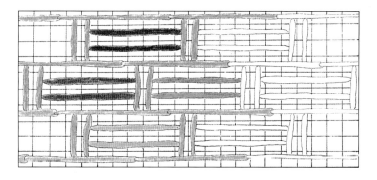

- White, cream or ecru shades of stranded cotton, soaked in a mixture of 50 per cent black tea and 50 per cent black coffee, to give an aged effect
- Sharp needle with an eye big enough to take four or more strands of cotton

Plushwork trees

See the instructions for working plushwork on pages 82–87.

Raised band stitch and chenille trees

You will need:

- Chunky chenille thread in foliage colours
- Brown stranded cotton or crewel wool for trunk
- Matching thread
- Pointed needles with eyes of appropriate sizes

This is a very simple, satisfying and effective way of creating trees against a wall.

Raised band stitch for tree trunk

First create horizontal rungs of foundation stitches across the width of the trunk. Start at the bottom left-hand side of the trunk and bring the needle up at 1. Move the needle to the right and, on the same horizontal canvas line, come down at 2 at the bottom right edge of the trunk. Now take the needle vertically underneath canvas and bring it up at 3 and so on.

Once you have all the rungs in place, you can start whipping the horizontal bars of the stitch. Starting from the left-hand side bring the needle up at the base and take it over and under the first bar, keeping the thread on the right. Continue doing this all the way up the tree trunk and plunge the thread down right on the top design line. With each progressive vertical row push the rows to the left with the eye of the needle to bunch the threads up, creating the raised band effect.

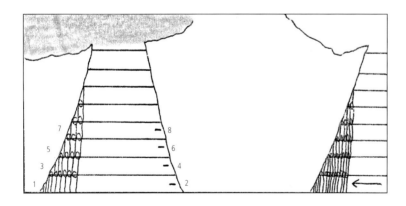

Chenille for tree foliage

Choose a chunky chenille thread and use a combination of colours if you wish. Zigzag the chenille across the space where the foliage of the tree will be represented and couch it down with a Gutermann thread in a similar colour.

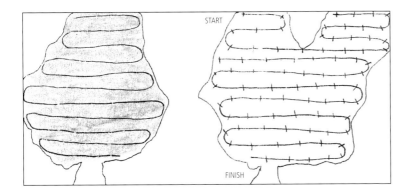

Below: Using chenille is a simple but effective way of creating trees against a wall.

Tab roses

To make the roses

First thread the needle with the cotton and knot one end. Cut two lengths of ribbon – one approximately 6cm (2.5in) and one 20cm (8in). Fold the 6cm (2.5in) length in half to create a loop. Hold the loop firmly in your right hand and lead the 20cm (8in) length of ribbon through the tab loop from the left at 90 degrees (A).

Fold the leading edge of the long ribbon around to the front of the tab loop so that it forms a little square. Secure the longer ribbon to the tab with a few stitches (B).

With the longer ribbon still running to the left, hold the lower end of the tab and twist it firmly clockwise so that the long ribbon wraps around itself to resemble a tight central bud of a rose. Secure the bud onto the tab with a few stitches (C).

To make the petals, leave a small distance from the bud, approximately 5–7.5mm (¼in) along the long ribbon. Fold the long ribbon backwards on itself so that the length falls away at a 90 degree angle (D).

Roll the bud clockwise towards the fold; this time leave the top of the roll looser to resemble a petal, but keep it tight at the base (E).

Secure the petal at the base with a few small stitches, making sure you pass the needle through the layers of ribbon and the tab so that it is really firm. Continue to form petals by folding, rolling and shaping until you have the size of rose you require.

Finally, cut off the excess length of the ribbon, leaving enough to fold back and oversew the raw edge. Turn the rose over and cut away the excess length of the tab. Oversew to neaten off, leaving a long length of thread attached with which to anchor the rose to the stem (F).

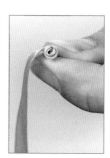

A   B   C   D   E   F   G

To anchor the roses

Scrunch up a small amount of foliage-coloured textured yarn, such as chenille, and push it onto the little platform of covered wire. Using a double thread, firmly oversew the yarn all around the wire platform. The stitches can be messy, as they will not show. Finish off with a double stitch on the surface and cut the thread.

Now take the thread you have left attached to the rose and put it into the needle. Plunge the needle straight down the centre of the 'foliage' on the wire platform and pull until the rose sits neatly on top. From the underneath, secure the rose into place with a few backstitches. You can put more than one rose on each platfom if you wish – three to six roses sitting together will look very effective (G).

To create the stems of the roses, take the wires that you have already covered in stranded cotton. Bring them all together at the base and stitch them together using a matching thread for as far as you require that thickness of stem. Bend the wire to give the impression of a realistic stem. As you progress upwards, allow some wires to run off in their own direction so that they 'ramble' over the wall. Create platform loops for rose bases as you go.

To finish off and mount the wall onto the canvas, see 121–122.

Below: Allow your roses to 'ramble' over the wall for a realistic effect.

Historical background

The art of English brick making was revived in the 13th and 14th centuries in the Eastern Counties largely due to a shortage of local stone and timber. However, fashion also influenced the growing popularity of this building medium, with ideas coming from Europe, especially the Hanseatic Ports in Northern Germany, where brickwork was extensively and imaginatively used for public and domestic buildings.

Tudor brick makers were recognised as craftsmen in their own right. Usually itinerant, they would work on a building site using wood or turf-fired clamps and local clay. With each firing the 'standard' handmade bricks were inevitably of a slightly different size, shape and colour. Some were deliberately burned to a deep purply-black; these were used to pick out a diaper or other patterns in the brickwork. Another technique was to elaborately twist the bricks for use in chimney pots such as the ones at Hampton Court Palace. When building the walls, thick mortar was used to even out the discrepancies between the size and shape of the bricks.

Porous walls that have no damp-proof course draw water from the surrounding soil into the brickwork and the damp travels upwards into the higher bricks. Over the centuries, the porous bricks begin to decay and break down, changing in colour and shape. Moss and algae inevitably appear on rough surfaces in the lower areas of the wall where the bricks are damper. Natural growth appears less frequently in higher areas, where often the natural salts from both bricks and mortar have been expelled, resulting in a bleached appearance.

Left: Mellow brickwork at Hatfield House, Hertfordshire, provides a backdrop for stunning topiary.

Appendix 1

Dressing a slate frame

There are two good reasons for using a slate frame:

1) The frame holds the entire area of the fabric at an even tension and so minimizes distortion of the work. Canvas is a loosely woven fabric, with no strength in the construction of the material. By securing the canvas on a frame, you are resisting random movement of the warp and weft threads.

2) Long-term projects can be stored safely on a slate frame.

Slate frames are usually made of beech, which is very strong and plentiful. They consist of two arms, with a staggered set of 16 small holes at each end, and two bars with webbing tape stapled along the length. At each end of the bars, there is an oval hole into which the arms fit snugly as the frame is constructed. Once the frame is made up to the required size, four split pins are wedged firmly into the small holes on the arms to hold the whole structure together securely.

Frames are usually sold in either 46cm (18in) or 61cm (24in) sizes. Note that this measurement relates to the length of webbing attached and not to the overall size of the frame.

If you follow these instructions accurately, you will achieve the primary purpose of using a slate frame – to maintain the tension of the canvas and prevent distortion during working. These instructions relate to a slate frame; if you are using a different type of frame with webbing tape, follow them until you reach the stage where the arms are attached.

Framing up is a slow process and will probably take about two hours, but it pays to be careful and work accurately.

You will need:

- Correct gauge (TPI) of canvas, measured and cut to size
- Tape measure
- HB pencil (never use a biro or other kind of pen while framing up)
- Pencil sharpener
- Glass-headed pins
- No. 14 yarn darner needle
- Buttonhole thread
- Large sacking or bracing needle (also known as curved spring needle)
- Ball of string
- Additional webbing tape (also known as upholstery webbing)
- Scissors

The size of your canvas

Your canvas should be narrower in width than the webbing tape on the bars of the frame. If your webbing tape is 61cm (24in), your canvas should be no wider than 46cm (18in) to leave 7.5cm (3in) on each side, from the edge of the canvas to the end of the webbing tape. This will leave a distance of about 10cm (4in) from the edge of the canvas to the arms; you will need this space to adjust the tension in the sides when you string up.

If your canvas is wider, you will need to cut it to size or purchase a larger frame. Do not fold your canvas vertically down each side to fit the width of your webbing as this will create an uneven tension.

Before you start to frame up, you must have already drawn your design on the canvas (see pages 25–26).

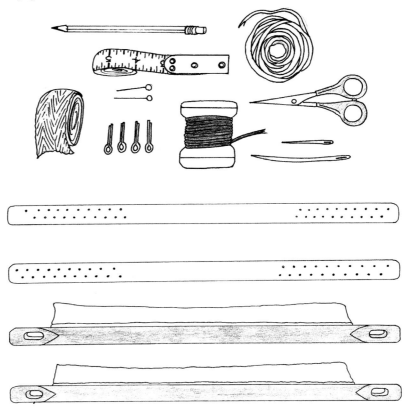

The first frame bar

Step 1

First, measure the webbing to find the centre mark: place the first bar on a flat surface and make sure the webbing flap is facing you. Measure the webbing tape from side to side along the free edge (the one that has not been stapled to the wood). You may find that the webbing has been folded over at each end, in which case measure from the edge of the fold. Using a pencil, accurately mark the centre of the webbing.

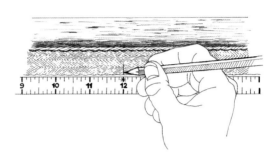

Step 2

Next, check the grain and centre measurements of the canvas: lay the canvas on a flat surface and find the centre measurement along the top width, which you will have marked when you were drawing on your design. At this stage, check again to make sure the canvas is cut accurately on the grain, both widthwise and lengthwise.

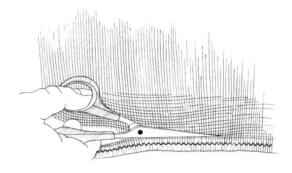

Step 3

With the centre mark visible and working from the top, fold the canvas back on itself horizontally to a depth of about 2.5cm (1in), making sure you keep the crease on the grain. Remember that the grain of the canvas is, in fact, the holes between the threads, so make sure your crease runs consistently between the same two horizontal threads. You have now created a hinge, which will strengthen the canvas once it is stitched onto the webbing.

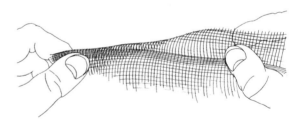

Step 4

Accurately place the canvas along the back of the webbing tape on the frame bar. To do this, hold the webbing tape up at 90 degrees from the frame bar so that the back of the tape is exposed. Place the crease of the canvas flush with the free edge of the webbing tape, so that the 2.5cm (1in) fold of the canvas lies against the back of the webbing tape and the cut edge of the canvas is parallel with the wooden bar. Accurately marry up the centre marks of the webbing tape and the canvas.

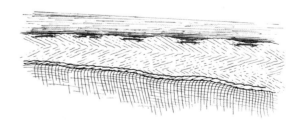

Step 5

You now have the canvas facing towards you, with the webbing at the back of the canvas. Starting from the centre mark, pin the canvas to the webbing, working out towards the left of the frame. (If you are left-handed, you may prefer to work out towards the right of the frame.) The pin should enter the two layers of canvas at the front of the work and go into the webbing tape away from you. Return it back through the tape and into the canvas on the right side. The pins should enter the top row of holes in the canvas and return about four rows down. They should stand straight and vertical at 2.5cm (1in) intervals along the webbing and canvas.

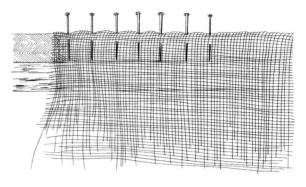

Step 6

Keeping the frame bar horizontal, turn it clockwise so that your pins are on the right-hand side; the canvas faces away from you and the webbing is nearest to you. Again, work from the centre towards the left of the frame and continue to enter the pin first through the canvas and then into the webbing so that this time the pins will be coming towards you, not away from you. You now have one frame bar pinned and are ready to stitch the canvas in place.

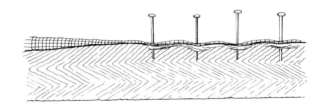

Step 7

Turn the frame again so that the canvas is facing you. Thread a No. 14 yarn darner with a length of buttonhole thread and tie a knot at one end. Place the needle near the top of the canvas centre point and pull it through the canvas and webbing so that the knot sits tightly on the canvas. Place the point of the needle near to the exit thread on the webbing tape and pull it through to the canvas side. Place the needle near the exit thread on the canvas side and return it to the webbing tape side. Repeat the process, ensuring that you finish on the canvas side. You have now created two small stab stitches, which will secure your knot.

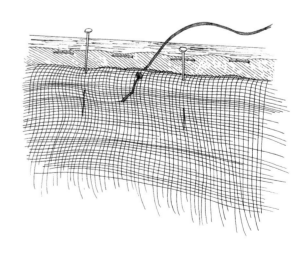

Step 8

The next stage is to stitch the first half of the canvas to the webbing tape. The stitch used is similar to oversewing. However, remember that canvas is a weakly woven fabric and if you were to use stitches of the same size along the grain of the fabric, this would have two unfortunate consequences. The first of these is that the even stitches would create a ridge, so the canvas could not lie flat against the webbing. Uneven tension would result. Secondly, the canvas would, in any event, rip away from the webbing tape as the frame was tightened and tension applied.

These problems are avoided by using a series of staggered long and short stitches, angled against the grain. Hold the canvas and the webbing flush and upright between your thumb and forefinger. Remember you are working from the centre towards the left. The needle and thread are on the canvas side, following the completion of the stab stitches.

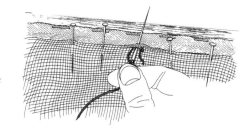

First short stitch – take the needle from the front of the canvas over to the back of the webbing tape. Place the needle near and to the left of your stab stitch and about 2mm (⅛in) only from the top of the webbing. Pass the needle horizontally, taking it straight through the layers of webbing and canvas, and pull the thread tight.

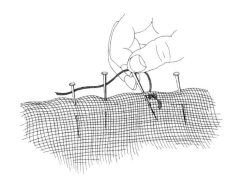

First long stitch – take the needle, again from the front of the canvas, over to the back of the webbing tape. Place it about 5mm (¼in) to the left of your first short stitch and take it through the webbing tape only. With the needle in position, raise the eye and angle the point to the left about 45 degrees. Pull the needle through about 1cm (½in) lower, bringing the thread through tightly to the front of the canvas as shown.

Take the needle to the back of the webbing tape, about 5mm (¼in) to the left of the first long stitch, and make a second short stitch. Continue with alternate long and short stitches until you reach the end of the canvas, removing any unwanted pins as you travel along.

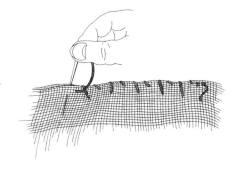

Step 9

To maximize the strength of your work, when you reach the end of the canvas work back about 5cm (2in) to the right using short stitches only. Finish off by cutting the thread close to the canvas.

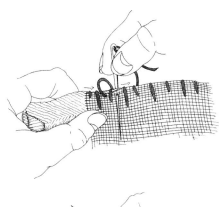

Step 10

To stitch the second half of the canvas to the webbing tape, turn the frame bar clockwise as before, so that the stitched side is to your right, the webbing tape is towards you and the canvas is facing away from you. Starting in the centre, create stab stitches as in step 7, but remember that this time your initial knot will lie on the webbing tape side and this is the side you will finish your stab stitches. Take your needle and thread from the front of the webbing tape over to the back of the canvas and create your first short stitch as in step 8.

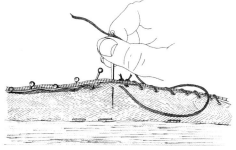

Take the needle and thread, again from the front of the webbing tape, over to the back of the canvas to create your first long stitch as in step 8, but this time you will put the point of the needle through the two layers of canvas only before you angle it up to come through the webbing tape lower down. Secure the ends of the canvas as in step 9.

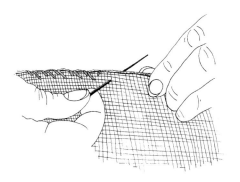

You now have your first frame bar completely stitched up. Repeat the process for the second bar.

The side arms

Step 11

Put the arms side-by-side on a flat surface and 'mirror image' the small holes at each end of the bars. Slide the arms through the large oval holes on the top and lower bars, ensuring that you keep the small holes mirror imaged so that when the split pins are inserted, the tension on the frame will be correct. Ensure that the arms are level with each other at top and bottom.

Step 12

Place two split pins into the small holes inside the top bar so that the pins rest against the bar. Ease the lower bar away from the top until the canvas is taut and you feel that you have the correct tension. Insert the remaining two split pins into the small holes inside the lower bar.

Recognizing the correct tension

It is not sufficient to create tension only on the top and lower bars. To stabilize the canvas completely, the sides must also be fixed at tension. To achieve this, we attach webbing tape down both sides of the canvas and then lace it to the arms of the frame with string. Webbing tape spreads the tension evenly across the work; if it were not used, you would find that a tension line would cut directly across the canvas at points where the string entered, and as tension was applied, the canvas would rip.

Recognizing the correct tension is largely a matter of experience, but the important point is that the canvas should be taut all over and stable between the four sides of the frame. (Remember that if you are applying suede or any other fabric as a path you will need to stitch the fabric in place on a slack frame, so that you can ultimately tighten both canvas and fabric up together to the same tension. See page 39.)

Step 13

Cut a length of webbing tape to fit the full drop, from top to bottom of the canvas. You will see that the tape has a herringbone pattern running vertically, and you will be able to use the centre herringbone line as a guide when placing the webbing against the canvas. Place the frame so that the front of the canvas is upwards and facing you, and start to work on the left-hand side.

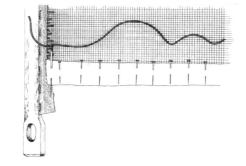

Place the webbing tape at the front of the canvas, with the centre herringbone line resting against the creased edge. Pin the tape to the canvas.

Step 14

You will use a basting stitch to attach the canvas to the webbing. Try to keep the depth of your stitches to about 1cm (½in) and ensure that the stitch never exceeds 2.5cm (1in). The stitches will run diagonally down the canvas and form a ridge as you pull them tight. Do not worry about this, as the ridge will pull out once you start the lacing.

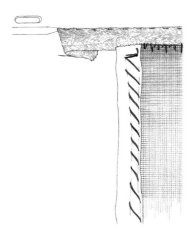

Cut a length of buttonhole thread. Try to judge the length so that you will be able to complete the stitching; if you run out of thread, however, just start again with a new length and a double stitch. Thread a No. 14 yarn darner as before and tie a knot in the end. Place the needle into the webbing tape at the top, 5mm (¼in) to the right of the centre herringbone line, so the needle also enters canvas. Pull the needle through the tape and canvas so that the knot rests on the top of the tape.

Take the needle horizontally to the right for about 1cm (½in) and bring it back up, taking it through both canvas and webbing. Take the needle back to the original point of entry and repeat the process so that you have a straight double stitch to secure the knot.

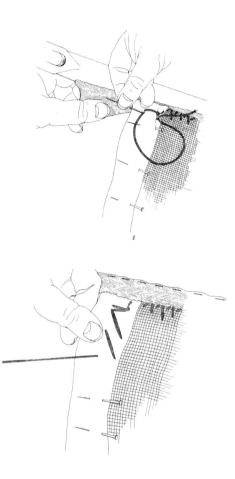

Take the needle across the tape so that it is about 1cm (½in) directly below the original point of entry. Pull the needle through the webbing and the canvas. Now move the needle down 1cm (½in) and bring it back through both layers. You are stitching in a zigzag, but the stitches will appear diagonal and parallel to each other on each side.

When you reach the end of the webbing, finish off with another horizontal double stitch.

Turn the frame around so that again you work on the left-hand side and repeat the process for the second side of the canvas.

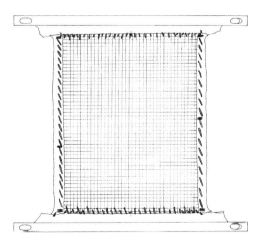

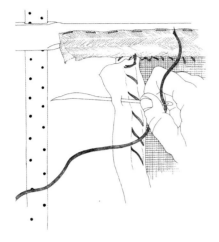

Step 15

Next, work the lacing from left to right along the webbing tape attached to the canvas. Thread a large sacking (bracing) needle with string. It is difficult to assess the amount of string you will need, so do not cut a length off, but keep it intact to the ball. Feed more string through the needle as you go and keep adjusting the length of string through the work. Stab the needle into the webbing tape at the top end and about 5mm (¼in) away from the free edge of the tape. Bring the string around the arm and back into the tape about 2.5cm (1in) from the original stitch. Continue working along the arm of the frame and into the webbing tape.

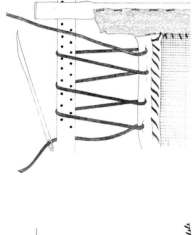

Lace the final arm in the same way, ensuring that you have the same number of loops on each side and that the lacing is mirror-imaged.

To secure each end of the string, wind it around the ends of the frame bars and tie with a slip knot.

Congratulations – your slate frame is professionally framed up and you are ready to start stitching.

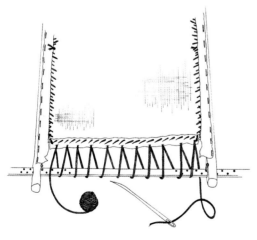

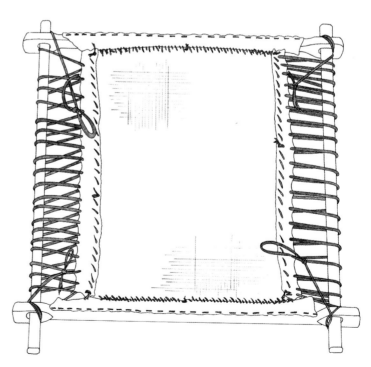

Appendix 2

Mounting a knot garden

You will need:

Read steps 1 to 3 before starting.

After you have spent many, many hours embroidering your knot garden, do make sure that is it properly mounted for display. Mounting should NOT involve staple guns, or gluing the canvas directly onto the card. The canvas should be mounted in a way that, if required in the future, it can be easily removed from the card for repair or conservation, and re-mounted again. The garden should be mounted in a way that complements the work and keeps all the embroidery intact and clearly visible.

It is satisfying to do the work yourself, but you will need hands of steel or a strong friend. The method we describe here is suitable for mounting a knot garden, but if in doubt, do seek professional advice or even get the work mounted by a professional embroiderer. It will be an investment and money well spent (see Suppliers page 125). Good preparation is always essential with any embroidery job and the end result will always be more pleasing and satisfying.

You will need:

- Grade A conservation card 3mm (⅛in) thick
- Cutting mat
- Craft knife
- Set square
- Steel rule
- Pencil and rubber
- Fabric glue
- Washed calico cut to size
- Wadding
- Curved needle
- Buttonhole thread
- Heavy-duty clean pins

Step 1
Measure the area to mount while the work is still on the slate frame. Draw out the area onto the card using a metal ruler and a sharp pencil, checking with a set square that your lines correspond. Cut along the lines on a cutting mat using a craft knife against a steel rule, making sure the cut is crisp and even.

Step 2
Wash the calico to remove the biological dressing put into the fabric and iron while it is still wet before use to ensure all creases are removed. This will create a better tension when mounting. Calico shrinks drastically when washed, so allow for this when estimating against the size of the board. You should also allow for at least a 10cm (4in) overlap on all sides.

Step 3
Lay the washed and ironed calico onto a flat surface. Place the card centrally onto the calico. You should have at least 10cm (4in) to fold over on all sides.

Starting with one side, glue a line parallel to the edge about 5cm (2in) on the card. Press the calico onto this and allow to bond. Turn the card around to the opposite side and repeat the process. Pull the calico so it lies tight and flat against the card. Do not force the calico as this might bend the card.

Step 4
Repeat the process on the remaining sides. Once fully dry cut any excess calico away to neaten the appearance.

Step 5
Turn the card over so the covered side faces you. Measure the four sides and mark the centre of each edge in pencil. Measure your knot garden to find the centre points of each edge and pin or tack a removable marker. This will enable you to place the garden squarely onto the board. Cut a thin piece of wadding (no more than 1cm (½in) thick) slightly smaller than the card and position it centrally onto the card.

If your garden has double facing brick walls go on to Brick Wall Mounting and come back to this stage later. Do not take your garden off the frame if you are going to mount brick walls. Only take your knot garden off the frame when you are ready to mount onto card without walls. Your work could distort if left off the frame for too long. Taking your knot garden off a frame must be done with care. First release the tension on the string by pulling the string and removing it from the frame.

Release the split pins, remove the arms and roll the upper and lower bars away from the work. Rest the work flat on a table to cut the stitches on the webbing tape and the canvas away. Find the end of the thread at one end of the frame and pull the thread gently back, undoing the stitches. Repeat this for both ends, releasing the work from the frame. Lay the knot garden onto the wadding, and line up the markers and pins on the board.

Step 6
Now pin the entire canvas to the card. To ease the tension from the canvas as you work, remove the pins in turn one at a time with a slight tug and put the pin back. Always work with the pins that are directly opposite one another (1).

With the work squarely on the board, position the pins around the board (2). When you pin work out onto a board always start

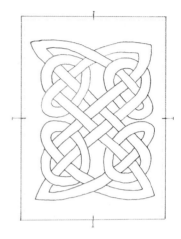

1

2

at the centre pin and work your way out towards the corners of the work area A. As you pin, keep the fabric on the grain. Go back to the centre and work your way across to the other corner, area B. Continue with areas C, D, areas E, F, and areas G, H. The arrows show the direction the tension will be pulled. When you have finished, ensure that the work is tight with no movement.

Now the work has been stretched you will need to turn it over. To avoid crushing your work if you have tall features in the garden you will need to build up soft walls of support to create a well for your garden to rest in. You can use pillows, cushions or rolls of bubble wrap. Whatever you do, it must be deep enough and wide enough to support the garden. The excess fabric must be cut away from the corners to even out the bulk on the back of the work. Do not cut right up to the corner; leave at least 1cm (½in). This will stop the fraying of the base fabric into the work (3).

3

Step 7

To lace the canvas at the back, use a long length of buttonhole or linen thread and secure into the canvas and calico with a small knot and two or three stab stitches. Start at A and lace the fabric, pulling on the thread to create the tension. Following the directions of the arrows, this will guide you as to where the thread enters the fabric, zig zagging it's way across the back of the work. If you run out of thread along the way, tie off using the same starting method. Finish off at B (4). Repeat the process on the remaining side (5).

4

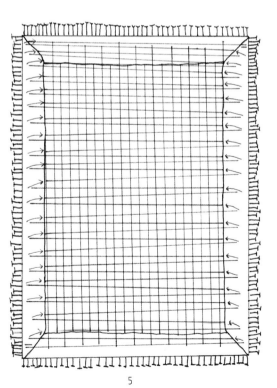

5

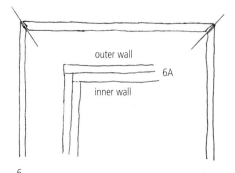

outer wall

inner wall

6A

6

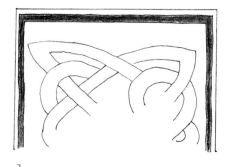

7

Step 8

Once the work has been laced take all the pins out and slip stitch a suitable backing fabric onto the board. To do this, cut a piece of fabric slightly smaller than the mount board and turn in all raw edges. Pin it onto the back of the laced canvas, making sure the fabric is on the grain. Slipstitch with buttonhole thread. For slip stitching see diagram 8 at overleaf.

Brick wall mounting

If you have brick walls to mount onto your garden, bear in mind that you must keep your knot garden on the slate frame as you will be stitching the brick walls through the canvas. Make sure all your panels are labelled clearly as to which inner panel and outer panels sit together.

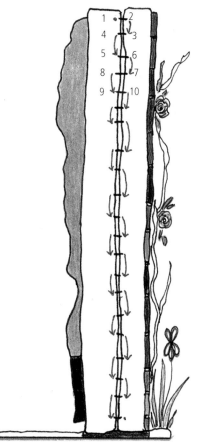

The outer walls should be slightly larger than the inside walls (6). The inner walls will lock into place with the outer wall creating a complete barrier (6A). The foundation area is where your brick walls will sit (7). You will need to allow for this space at a very early stage in the designing of the knot garden. The area should measure the width of your brick walls, allowing for thickness of card, bulk of canvas and both the visible stitching and the lacing. A very simple backstitch using a green crewel or 4 ply knitting yarn can be used to flood the foundation area with simple stitches, making sure no canvas is visible and that the stitches are not too long. If you choose not to include the walls then this area can be lost within the mounting of the garden at a later stage. Go back to step 5 of Mounting to mount each individual wall (see page 120).

Step 9

Once the walls have been individually mounted, position the inner wall centrally to the outer wall and slipstitch in place (8). Use a curved needle and a strong

8

buttonhole thread. Follow the number sequence and follow the wall all the way around. To disguise any bare canvas, continue the brick pattern and oversew the edges with a curved needle and a suitable blend of stranded cottons.

Bring all the slipstitched pieces together. Check their length and width against the stitched foundation area. Position the walls as you would like to see them and stitch all the corners with buttonhole thread, bringing the piece together to form a square. Place the square onto the garden and pin into position. With a heavy-duty needle and buttonhole thread, carefully stitch the brick wall in place. Bring the needle up at an angle away from the brick wall on the outside and angle the needle into the edge of the wall on the way down. Repeat this for the inside wall.

9

Step 10

Most Tudor brick walls had a capping stone placed on them to minimise the effects of weathering. If you want to add a capping stone (9) to your brick wall follow the instructions below.

Measure the length and width of the top of each brick wall. Cut a strip of card exactly to these measurements and cover with a suitable linen or calico that has been made dirty. Lace the fabric onto the card and position with the laced side against the top of the wall. Repeat this on all walls around garden (10).

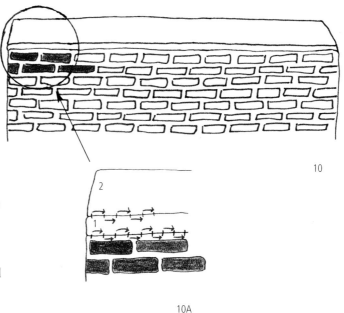

10

10A

The capping stone in the original knot garden is a piece of small wood moulding bought from a toyshop. I've cut the wood at an angle at the corners to create a neat mitre. The moulding was covered and stitched in the same way as the card (10A).

Slipstitch the card top or the moulding onto the wall using a curved needle and buttonhole thread. Now you can take your work out of the frame and mount the main garden. Use the brick walls as a support and mount as explained in Mounting, steps 1–8 (see pages 119–121).

Recommended further reading

Chapter two

HISTORY
Beck, Thomasina, *Gardening in Silk and Gold: A History of Gardens in Embroidery*, David and Charles
Blomfield, Reginald, *The Formal Garden in England*, Timber Press
Campbell-Culver, Maggie, *The Origin of Plants*, Headline
Field, Robert, *Mazes Ancient and Modern*, Tarquin
Strong, Roy, *The Renaissance Garden in England*, Thames and Hudson
Thomas Etty Esq., Heritage Bulb Merchant and Seedsman – Annual Seed Catalogue contains
    list of plants used through the centuries
Uglow, Jenny, *A Little History of British Gardening*, Chatto and Windus
Whalley, Robin and Jennings, Anne, *Knot Gardens and Parterres*, (part 1), Barn Elms

INSPIRATION
Beck, Thomasina, *The Embroiderer's Garden*, David and Charles
Don, Monty and Sarah, *The Jewel Garden*, Hodder and Stoughton (for exciting descriptions
    of how one garden changes its personality week by week throughout the year)
Hemphill, John and Rosemary, *The Fragrant Garden*, Bookmart Ltd
Lloyd, Christopher, *Colour for Adventurous Gardeners*, BBC Books
National Gardens Scheme, *The Yellow Book*. Published annually (see also www.ngs.org.uk)
Pope, Nori and Sandra, *Colour by Design*, Conran Octopus

TECHNICAL
Whalley, Robin and Jennings, Anne, *Knot Gardens and Parterres* (part 2), Barn Elms.
    Good for help on drawing out designs

Chapters three and four
Eriksson, Helen, *Ribbon Renaissance – Artistry in Silk*, Sally Milner Publishing
Franklin, Tracy and Jarvis, Nicola, *Contemporary Whitework*, Batsford
Franklin, Tracy, *New Ideas in Goldwork*, Batsford
Rhodes, Mary, *Dictionary of Canvas Work Stitches*, Batsford
Hill, Penny, *Knitting*, Sunburst

Chapter seven
Field, Robert, *Geometric Patterns from Tiles and Brickwork*, Tarquin
Lloyd, Nathaniel, *A History of English Brickwork*, Antique Collectors' Club, 1999

Suppliers

For updated lists of suppliers and further information on knot garden workshops, please visit www.embroideredknotgardens.com

General supplies

For general supplies, including canvas, Appletons crewel wool and slate frames:

The Royal School of Needlework
Apt 12A Hampton Court Palace
Surrey KT8 9AU
Tel: 020 8943 1432
Email: sales@royal-needlework.co.uk
www. royal-needlework.co.uk

Your knot garden can be professionally mounted by staff in the Studio at the Royal School of Needlework

Address and telephone number as above.
Email: enquiries@royal-needlework.co.uk

Specialist threads

Oliver Twists
22 Phoenix Road
Crowther,
Washington
Tyne and Wear
NE38 0AD
Tel: 0191 4166016
Email: jean@olivertwists.freeserve.co.uk

Stef Francis
Waverley
Higher Rocombe
Stokeinteignhead
Newton Abbot
Devon TQ12 4QL
Tel: 01803 323004
Email: sales@stef-francis.co.uk
www.stef-francis.co.uk

For all embroidery supplies, visit the annual autumn knitting and stitching shows at the NEC, Birmingham; Alexandra Palace, London; RDS, Dublin; and the International Centre, Harrogate. For further details contact:

Creative Exhibitions Ltd
8 Greenwich Quay
Clarence Road
London SE8 3EY
Tel: 020 8692 2299
Email: mail@twistedthread.com
www.twistedthread.com

Recommended gardens to visit

For details of Botanic Gardens in Britain please contact:

Royal Botanic Gardens
Kew
Richmond
Surrey TW9 3AB
Tel. 020 8940 1171
www.rbgkew.org.uk

The National Botanic Garden
of Wales
Llanarthne
Carmarthenshire SA32 8HG
Tel: 01558 668768
www.gardenofwales.org.uk

Royal Botanic Garden Edinburgh
20A Inverleith Row
Edinburgh EH3 5LR
Tel: 0131 552 7171
www.rbge.org.uk

Botanic Gardens
College Park
Botanic Avenue
Belfast
Tel: 028 032 0202 ext.3438
www.belfastcity.gov.uk

For details of Royal Horticultural
Society Gardens:

Royal Horticultural Society
80 Vincent Square
London SW1P 2PE
Tel: 020 7834 4333
www.rhs.org.uk

For National Garden Scheme Visiting
in England, Scotland and Wales,
Australia, Japan and the USA

The National Garden Schemes
Charitable Trust
Hatchlands Park
East Clandon
Surrey GU4 7RT
Tel: 01483 211535

Museum of Garden History
Lambeth Palace Road
London SE1 7LB
Tel: 020 7401 8869
www.cix.co.uk

Gardens mentioned in this book:

The Abbey House Gardens
Malmesbury
Wiltshire SN16 9AS
Tel: 01666 822212
www.abbeyhousegardens.co.uk

Great Dixter
Northiam
Rye
East Sussex TN31 6PH
Tel: 01797 252878
www.greatdixter.co.uk

Hampton Court Palace
East Molesey
Surrey KT8 9AU
Tel: 020 8781 9500
www.hrp.org.uk

Hatfield House
Hatfield
Hertfordshire AL9 5NQ
www.hatfield-house.co.uk

Levens Hall
Kendal
Cumbria LA8 0PD
Tel:015395 60321
www.levenshall.co.uk

Pollok House
2060 Pollokshaws Road
Glasgow G43 1AT
Tel: 0141 6166410
www.clyde-valley.com

Sissinghurst Castle
North Cranbrook
Kent TN17 2AB
Tel. 01580 710700
www.nationaltrust.org.uk

Acknowledgements

We are grateful to the very many students, colleagues and friends who have inspired and contributed their knowledge and experience to the writing of this book. We are sorry we cannot mention them all, but special thanks must go from both of us to:

The staff at Batsford, Tina Persaud and Kristy Richardson for their patient support throughout this project, and Michael Wicks for his sharp photographic eye. Artist Nicola Jarvis for her beautiful drawings interspersed throughout the book, for being there then and now and for being a great friend. International Photographer Nicola Kurtz whose input was greatly appreciated. The staff of the Lindley Library, the staff of Surbiton Library, and Chris Crowder – Head Gardener at Levens Hall. Elizabeth Elvin, Principal of the Royal School of Needlework for her encouragement and use of the School's facilities. Dora Brammer for continuing the tradition.

Anne Butcher, who in 1991 as Head of the Commercial Studios at the RSN recognised potential in the first male apprentice embroiderer at the School, and later introduced him to a class called 'Embroidered Gardens' as her teaching assistant. Andrew Calloway for his canvas work, Margaret Dier for her contemporary garden and Trudy Wilson for her enthusiastic support. Eva Hansson for help with the RSN Collection. Thanks also to Barbara and Ian Pollard.

Especial thanks to the inspiring students who have allowed their work to be photographed; Gillian Allen, Pat Butler, Elizabeth Button, Susie Carnegie, Sheila Cockerton, Carolyn Enfield, Ann Esslemont, Janice Hunt, Amanda Jillings, Helen Parkinson, Judith Pooley, Louise Reboul, Viv Roberts, Carol Stewart and Maggy Stonebridge.

Our thanks for their unswerving support to Iris and Brian Davies, Owen's sisters Tracy and Lesley and the Three Little Roses, nieces Lucy, Ellen and Hannah; John Leahy for his support and the use of his beautiful garden; Dick Holdsworth for regular meals, courier service and the use of his computer; Isabel Holdsworth for help with the manuscript; Alison Holdsworth, Richard Lanning and Ashley and Alan Patterson for their amused disbelief and helpful suggestions; Tracy Franklin for her fine example and advice; Pat Healy for the generous use of her house and equipment; Jill Russell for sanctuary during the final push; Ceri Williams for encouraging advice at just the right moments; Monica Wright for patient listening, practical help and being there from start to finish.

Finally our thanks to Hampton Court Palace for being such a beautiful and inspiring environment in which to work.

Owen Davies and Gill Holdsworth
December 2005

Index

brick walls 95
brickwork planning 99
    scrutiny of 95
brickwork stitch 47, 102
bullion knots 58

canvaswork 40
canvas types 11
colour choices 28
    examples 28–35
cornered chain stitch 54
cross oblong double tied
    stitch 51
cushion stitch 45

design considerations 14
design of paths and transfer
    to canvas 25
design storyboard 22
design tools 13

embroidery frames,
    preparation of 110
    ring 10
    slate/tent 9
    supports 10
encroaching straight
    stitch 55
eyelet circular variation
    stitch 57

fan stitch (ray stitch) 49, 57
flowerbeds 49
flower stitches 52
fountains, jet, knotted 71
    wired 72
French knot 47, 60

garden paths 37
gardens, real 6

suggested for visit 126
history, need to know 6
graph paper 25

Hampton Court Palace 27,
    95
heirloom, embroidered knot
    garden as 23
    sampler as 23
hedging and topiary 79
    choice of wools 80
    shaping 87
    trimming 85
historical backgrounds,
    brickwork 109
    hedging plants 88
    knot gardens 27
    plants 69
    topiary 92
    water 76
houndstooth stitch 50
    variation 51
hungarian stitch 46

knitting 68
knot garden, Hampton
    Court Palace 27
knot garden, mounting 119

labyrinths 15
Law, Ernest 27
Levens Hall 92, 126
lightbox 13
    improvised 13
    use of 26
lighting 13

materials 9
    canvas 11
    needles 11

slate frame 9
    preparation of 111
mazes 15
mortar stitch 102
mounting brick wall 122
    knot garden 119

national gardens scheme 126
needles 12
    chenille 40
needlelace leaves 62

paths 25, 37, 39
    design and transfer to
        canvas 25
plushwork, simple 82
    anchor stitch 83
    trees 104
pompons 88
postcards 14

raised band stitch 104
ray stitch (fan stitch) 57
ribbon work (irises) 64
rice stitch 53
ring frame 10
roses, tab 106

sampler 10, 23
satin balloon stitch 56
scissors 13
stitches,
    brickwork 47, 102
    bullion knots 58
    choice of 26
    cross oblong double
        tied 51
    cushion 45
    fan stitch see ray stitch
    flower stitches 52

French knot 47, 60
half cross 43, 49
houndstooth 50
    variation 51
hungarian 46
mortar 102
plushwork, simple 82
    anchor 83
    trees 104
    raised band 104
ray or fan 57
ribbonwork (irises) 64
rice 53
roses, tab 106
satin balloon stitch 56
tent 43
    woven picot 61
stitching technique 42
slate frame, 9
    dressing 110
stumpwork, woven picot 61

tab roses 106
tapestry, distinguished
    from embroidery 40
tent stitch 43, 49
threads, types, 12
    combination 12
    stranded cotton 37
    wool unsuitable for
        garden path 37
tracing paper 13
trees, securing to canvas 91
    creation from chenille 100,
        104
    plushwork 104

water features 71
    fountains 71, 72
    other water features 73